The
4 Laws
of
Financial
Prosperity

Get Control of
Your Money Now!

Just five words spell prosperity, success, and happiness—
five words only—and they are these:
"Spend less than you get."
—Anonymous

When prosperity comes, do not use all of it.
—Confucius

The
4 Laws
of
Financial
Prosperity

*Get Control of
Your Money Now!*

Blaine Harris
and Charles Coonradt

The
Financial
Wellness Group

The Financial Wellness Group™
P.O. Box 236
Bountiful, UT 84011-0236
1-800-245-6283
www.thefinancialwellnessgroup.com

Co-published by Franklin Covey Co.

ISBN 978-1-933976-86-0

Library of Congress Catalog Number: 96-085208

Printed in the United States of America

Introduction

When Paul Smith can't pay his bills, including minimum payments on five credit cards, a home equity loan, a first mortgage, and a car lease, he takes a midnight stroll seeking answers to his financial woes.

Fate and a strange set of events brings him in contact with Mary Sessions, a retired IRS auditor with a $20 million bank account who takes Paul into her home, dangles a $2 million carrot in front of his nose and begins teaching him the four laws that made her debt-free and financially secure.

Inspired by actual events, Paul discovers that how much a person earns isn't nearly as important in achieving financial security as most people think—that nearly anyone on any income can achieve debt-free peace and prosperity by applying the four laws in the story.

Taking place over a period of months, the reader accompanies Paul as Mary guides him, one step at a time, down the path leading to debt-free prosperity. By the time the surprise ending unfolds, the reader, along with Paul, has mastered the laws that can guide anyone down the same path.

Through an entertaining and captivating story, this book presents the four time-tested laws developed by Blaine Harris for The Financial Wellness Group in its financial management programs for individuals, families, students, employees, and business owners—making a difference for you and your loved ones today and tomorrow.

The Next Move Is Yours!

*Successful men and women become
successful only because they acquire the habit
of thinking in terms of success.*

*Definiteness of purpose can, and it should,
so completely occupy the mind that one has no time or space
in the mind for thoughts of failure.*
—Napoleon Hill

Dedication

to those who will commit to become
financially free

Acknowledgments

I would like to acknowledge several people who have had a profound impact upon my life. I would not have understood the fundamental concepts of this book with a deep enough passion to make this project an international reality without help from the following:

First to my parents, who are no longer here, for teaching me that personal integrity is inseparably connected to accountability and responsibility.

To my wife, Elaine, for her unquestioning faith and support for this work and everything else I am involved in.

To my children, for testing, implementing, and further documenting the principles taught in this book.

To my daughter Marci and son-in-law Ken, for their undying loyalty and ongoing assistance in the development of our Financial Wellness products and services.

To our staff, who have spent countless hours to support and develop the refinements reflected in this book.

To our international friends and clients, who have patiently and enthusiastically proven the flexibility and durability of these principles.

To Mr. Chuck Coonradt, who developed *The Game of Work* and who contributed much to the preparation of this book.

To Lee Nelson, whose writing skill and belief in the 4 Laws process enabled us to present the concepts and principles in this book in an easy-to-read and enjoyable format.

—*Blaine Harris*

Acknowledgments

I want to thank my partner—that is my life partner, business partner, parenting partner, and eternal partner—my wife, Carla, without whom my life would not have turned out the way it has.

Also thanks to my children, Christina, Kelly, Christopher, Cody, and Christian—without you, none of this would have been possible or very important.

Thank you to the thousands of chief executive officers and owners who have retained and used our concepts. These people hired us to teach and, in fact, wound up teaching me.

Thanks to Blaine Harris, for his vision and commitment to the timeless principles of the 4 Laws—and for his invitation to be a part of this great work.

—*Charles Coonradt*

Contents

A fluctuating economy with interest rates that are continually changing is part of life. As such, in any given year, the lending rates and rates of return used for illustration purposes in this book may be higher or lower than the current market. However, the principles taught are timeless and will benefit your life as you apply them with consistency and diligence. We commend you for your dedication to building greater financial health, balance and strength. It will pay you many times over throughout your life and the life of your family! (Note: The rate of return used on investment savings is based on historical averages).

Foreword

by Dr. Stephen R. Covey

This profound little book deals with a topic that is absolutely critical to quality of life for everyone. No matter who you are or where you live, for most of your life you will deal with economic issues. And these issues not only affect the amount of money you have in your wallet, your bank account, or your 401k; they also affect your relationships, your lifestyle choices, your levels of stress, your ability to contribute, and your personal peace.

That's why, as the authors say in their Introduction, the issue really isn't one of how much money you make. It's one of "financial peace and prosperity"—of reaching a point where money becomes an enabler, not a distractor, from the things that really matter most in your life.

I found *The 4 Laws of Financial Prosperity* to be truly unique and inspiring in several ways.

It's based on a "whole life" approach.

This book recognizes that financial wellness is an integral part of happiness and well-being. Unlike other books on the market, it's not reactive. It doesn't just focus on how to get out of debt. It's not incomplete and short-sighted. It doesn't just focus on strategies and techniques to increase wealth. It's about your whole life. It helps you tie your financial goals into your deepest values and principles. It helps you handle your money in a way that enables you to accomplish what really matters most.

It strikes at the "root" of money problems.

Even as I write this foreword, we're in the midst of a global economic crisis. We're struggling to deal with the consequences of the quick-fix, easy-credit mentality that led to a meltdown of the subprime mortgage market in the United States and the fallout of that meltdown around the globe. But as challenging as this crisis is, it's really only one of the "fruits" of a much deeper "root"—this mentality of trying to accumulate and "manage" money essentially for the purpose of amassing wealth. This way of thinking disregards the timeless principles that govern the purpose, use, and management of resources to create happiness and well-being. *The 4 Laws of Financial Prosperity* addresses the "root" of some of the "fruits" we're experiencing because of a nonprincipled approach.

It's based on timeless principles.

Like the 7 Habits, the 4 Laws distill complex ideas and processes into simple, actionable principles of effectiveness. Anyone can follow these laws—Track, Target, Trim, and Train—and get positive results. The 4 Laws also embody many of the 7 Habits themselves—especially Habit 1: Be Proactive, Habit 2: Begin With the End in Mind, Habit 3: Put First Things First, and Habit 7: Sharpen the Saw. In fact, the 4 Laws even get into the 8th Habit, helping people move from effectiveness to greatness. They increase your ability to not only enjoy fulfillment in your daily life, but to be in a position to contribute time, energy, and resources in other areas as well.

It's a great tool to increase organizational productivity.

Having spent my career helping individuals and corporations increase productivity, I've become convinced that one of the greatest, unnoticed drains on individual productivity is the distraction that financial stress puts on people. When up to 50 percent of employees spend 21 or more hours at work each month dealing with the stress of personal financial issues, it can't help but affect their focus, decision making, relationships, and creativity. This is a great little book to help employees achieve financial wellness and increase organizational performance at the same time.

It's written in an easy-to-read, engaging style.

Not only is the book sound; it's engaging and easy to read—which is rare in the world of money-management literature. The story line makes the logic memorable and easy to follow, yet it doesn't get in the way of helping us understand that the principles are applicable for all.

Blaine and Chuck do a great job of inspiring us and helping us understand that financial wellness is both desirable and achievable. One of the things I like best about the book is that not only are the principles true, they are easy to apply and bring immediate as well as long-term results. Members of my own family have enjoyed and learned from this book. I believe you will too.

Whatever you can do or dream you can, begin it.
Boldness has genius and magic in it.
Begin it now.
—Goethe

Do not let what you cannot do interfere with what you can do.
—John Wooden,
former UCLA basketball coach

Money is plentiful for those who understand the
simple laws which govern its acquisition.
—George Clason

A Lady Named Mary

The Paul Smith Story

It was almost midnight when I went looking for a way out, or at least something to take my mind away from my bills. The dead of night has a way of making some problems seem unbearable. It was the worst night of my life. I could not sit at the desk another minute.

I wasn't in the midst of a life-and-death struggle with cancer, nor was I embroiled in a nasty divorce. My circumstances were more mundane but, to me, every bit as painful as any life-and-death struggle.

It was the time of the month when I had to spend an evening at my desk paying bills. The evening had started out on a painful note when I examined a yellow card from the post office informing me that I had a registered letter from the IRS. I didn't cheat on my taxes, but was worried I had been a little too creative. I was a sales rep for a furniture manufacturer and always seemed to be spending personal money on business without getting receipts. At tax time, I usually gave myself a generous

1

deduction to cover these undocumented expenses. Now I was sure they were going to audit me, and even if they told me I had to come up with another $2,000 or go to jail, I wouldn't be able to find $2,000. Pushing the yellow card to the back of the desk, hoping it might get lost, I prayed the custodian at the IRS would inadvertently push my file into a wastebasket.

Then I started the gruesome task of paying bills, beginning with the small ones.

I made minimum payments on the five charge cards, trying to ignore the late fees and the small print describing finance charges of 18% to 25% on the unpaid balances.

I made an interest-only payment on the home equity loan, then examined a rejection letter from the company where I had applied for a second home equity loan. I had responded to their advertising, which claimed: "If you need money, get it out of your house. We give 100%, not 80% like those other home equity companies!" In the rejection letter, they said they couldn't make the loan because I didn't have sufficient income to make the payments. I threw the letter in the trash wondering about the banker mentality—the more you needed money the less they were inclined to loan it to you. It didn't seem fair that money is always more available to those who don't seem to need money.

Then I opened the letter from the vehicle leasing company announcing the lease on my car was finished. I was supposed to turn it in to the leasing dealer along with a check for $1,867 to cover the high-mileage penalty. This made me mad. My lease payments were higher than monthly purchase payments would have been, and now I owed almost $2,000 extra. How would I ever find enough money for a down payment on a new car? I was trapped.

In the pile of bills, I found a glimmer of hope. Through a cellophane window on the front of one of the envelopes, I could see my name and address printed on a check. I ripped it open.

It was a check for $1,500. Who would be sending me that kind of money?

A Lady Named Mary

A car dealer. The letter said I could use the check as part of the down payment on a new vehicle. Of course, in order to validate it, I had to show it to the sales manager before I started dealing on the new car. I knew their game. Raise the price $1,500, then send out $1,500 checks to all the suckers like me. I threw the check in the trash.

I paid all the utility bills, but I didn't have enough to make the house payment. I had initiated an overdraw feature on my checking account six months earlier so the bank would automatically cover overdrafts, but I was already over the $2,000 limit, was paying 18% on the balance, and would have to start making payments on that next month. I had used the last of the overdraw credit to make the house payment the month before, so I couldn't use the overdraft to make the current house payment.

I got up from the desk and tiptoed into the bedroom where my wife, Judy, was sleeping. Without turning on the light, I felt around in the bottom of the closet for our file box that contained the password master sheet for our online accounts. I returned to my desk to log into Judy's checking account, hoping she might have enough balance to cover the house payment.

I wasn't surprised to find no balance at all. Like me, she made purchases using her debit card, hoping she didn't overdraw the account. She sold real estate, and the spring months had been slow. It had been more than thirty days since her last commission, leaving her account in the same dire place as mine.

Tucked in the small compartment on top of the file box was a piece of white paper, folded up tight with the corner exposed. I pulled it out and unfolded it. My motivation wasn't so much curiosity as the need to do something, anything, in an effort to control my growing nightmare.

The paper was a receipt from one of those expensive boutique shops that lures its unsuspecting victims in to browse. The purchased item listed on the receipt was an artificial Christmas tree.

How well I remembered that tree, and the trauma it had

brought into my life at Christmastime. At first, Judy had brought home a live tree. After two nights of unsuccessful attempts to get me to string the lights on it, she expressed her frustration by going to the boutique and charging $200 on her VISA card to buy that artificial tree with the lights already in place. I was furious, but the tree stayed.

Now as I looked at the receipt, I realized Judy had deceived me. Yes, she had charged $200 on the VISA. She had also given the store a check for $200 and another $200 in cash. She had paid $600 for the tree! And she had disguised the price by splitting up the payment. She normally didn't do things like this. Apparently, putting lights on the tree had been a lot more important to her than I had supposed. I had been insensitive to her needs and deserved the punishment she had dished out—a $600 Christmas tree. It seemed I hadn't done anything right lately.

I headed into the garage to get the double-edged lumber axe. It was in the corner with the garden tools. Without putting on the safety goggles, I turned on the grinder and sharpened both edges. Boy, was Judy going to be sorry.

The artificial tree was in one of the plywood cabinets in the garage. I dragged it onto the front lawn and chopped it into little pieces. When there was nothing bigger than six inches, I buried the axe into the little sycamore tree we had been nursing along. Then I decided to take a walk before I did something really dangerous.

My head was a little calmer now. Swinging the big axe had helped, but none of my financial problems had gone away. The stupidity of what I had just done was settling in and so was the reality of our difficult financial situation. I needed to find some money, or my life would be in shambles.

I remembered thinking when I had graduated from college, I would have a great life if I worked hard and increased my earnings to about $70,000 a year. That was my dream, and I had achieved it. With commissions and bonuses, my income ranged from $68,000 to $75,000 a year, yet I couldn't afford to buy a wreath for my own funeral. I was wasting a $600 Christmas tree in the middle of the night because I couldn't pay my bills and was more miserable than I had been in my entire life. What was wrong? Where could I find the money to get out of this terrible predicament?

As I walked, I had an idea to go back home, draft a letter to my boss outlining all of the reasons I deserved a substantial pay raise and demand that if I didn't get it, effective immediately, she could consider the letter my resignation notice. Dumb idea! I needed the income, liked my job, and knew that with the current economic climate a raise of any kind was not in the cards. I kept walking.

It was long past midnight, and only one other house in the neighborhood had lights on.

As I walked up Maple Street, I could see an elderly woman through one of the front windows. She was sitting in an overstuffed chair, reading something. The name on the mailbox was M. Sessions. Her first name was Mary. I didn't know her well, only that she had a full-time gardener. She drove a late-model Mercedes, and sometimes chauffeurs picked her up. She lived alone in a house that would appraise for more than half a million dollars. I guessed she was in her late sixties or early seventies. In my occasional conversations with her, she had seemed friendly and articulate.

The thought occurred to me that maybe Mrs. Sessions would loan me some money. Reflecting back on our conversations over the years, I wished I had taken the time to get to know her better. But, at this moment, there was no time for building a strong, lasting friendship. I needed money now. Mustering courage, I tiptoed onto the porch and knocked on the door. I took a step back from the door, smiled and waved my hand slightly so she could recognize me from the image captured by her porch security camera.

"Nice to know I'm not the only one who can't sleep," she said brightly, asking if Judy and the kids were okay as she opened the door.

The 4 Laws of Financial Prosperity

There was an elegant quality about Mary Sessions. Even though her neatly-cropped hair was gray, there was a vibrant, healthy look about her. Her eyes were the color of Navajo turquoise, and had an intense, piercing quality rarely seen. She had fewer wrinkles than women half her age, even in the middle of the night with no makeup.

I asked her if she had a padded cell in her house.

"What in the world for?" she asked, laughing. I was pleased that she found my comment funny. Quickly, in my mind, I condensed my financial predicament and blurted it out, ending with, "If I don't find some money fast, I think I might just turn myself over to the local jailer, because that's where they'll be putting me if I can't pay my bills."

There was a lighthearted tone in my voice as I made this last statement. I didn't want her to think I was really serious, but deep down in my heart, I wasn't sure if I wouldn't land in jail.

"You are asking me for a loan?" she asked.

"Yes, I think money would be better than jail."

"I have never loaned money to a neighbor before," she said, hesitating. "But I suppose there's a first time for everything. Would you like to come in?" Pushing the door all the way open, she stepped back, allowing me to enter.

"Mr. Smith, how much do you need?" she asked.

"Please call me Paul. I think ten thousand would stop the bleeding," I said, suddenly wishing I hadn't said it, feeling ashamed at my audacity for dropping such a request at one in the morning on a 70-year-old woman I hardly knew.

She began to laugh.

"What's wrong?" I asked.

"Nothing," she said. "I'm just relieved. A neighbor shows up in the middle of the night asking for a padded cell or money, so I naturally assume he needs some real money, not just pocket change. Glad I was wrong."

Who was this woman who thought ten thousand dollars was pocket change?

A Lady Named Mary

"Twenty thousand would stop the bleeding and put a nice dressing on the wound," I said, suddenly feeling greedy enough to double my request.

"First you ask for ten, then for twenty. Sounds like you really don't know how much you need," she said. "No wonder the bank wouldn't give you money."

I had the sick feeling I had just blown a wonderful opportunity. I should not have been greedy.

"How did you know the bank wouldn't give me money?" I asked, suspecting that perhaps she owned the bank.

"Just a hunch," she winked. "Would you like to play some chess while we work this out?"

My idea of fun did not include playing chess in the middle of the night with a woman old enough to be my mother. But if a little chess would get me a loan, why not?

"Sure," I said, with pretended enthusiasm. We seated ourselves on sofas at opposite ends of a coffee table. The playing board and pieces were already in place. I decided to let her win, thinking that might improve my chances of getting the money.

We hadn't been playing very long when she went over to a desk, shuffled through one of the drawers, then returned with a little book in her hand. It was a register for a savings account.

"Most of my money is in stocks, bonds, and real estate," she explained, "but I keep a little bit in a savings account for emergencies." She tossed the register on the table in front of me, nodding for me to look inside. I did so, carefully memorizing the balance: $147,952.34.

"I suppose your coming here could be considered an emergency," she offered.

"It is for me," I said, very sincerely, still holding onto the register, hardly daring to hope that Mary Sessions might actually give me money.

As we continued the game of chess, I realized I didn't have to let her win. She was going to win whether I wanted to let her or not.

"Look," she said thoughtfully, when we were almost finished, "I don't like throwing good money after bad."

My hopes sank into the bottom of my shoes. She wasn't going to give me the money after all.

"I would feel a lot better about loaning you money if I thought it would do some good," she countered.

"Oh, it will," I assured her. "I'll make my house payment; buy hamburger and potatoes for the children to eat. None of it will be spent frivolously."

"You probably think I'm a silly old widow with more money than sense," she said.

"Oh no," I lied, wondering how she could read my mind.

"We were a month behind on the rent when my husband died," she said, suddenly changing the direction of our conversation. She leaned back, forgetting the chess game.

"I'm sorry."

"I don't need your sympathy, not anymore. I had three small children, no insurance, no savings, and no marketable skills. Do you have any idea what it is like getting food for your children in the trash bins behind grocery stores? When the clerks caught me, I told them I was looking for produce for my pet pig."

I couldn't believe what I was hearing. I tried hard to picture this elegant woman foraging through trash bins in search of food scraps for her babies. I couldn't imagine.

"But, what about all this?" I asked, pointing to the expensive surroundings and the register. "How did you get from there to here? And don't tell me you worked really hard. I know a lot of people who work hard and never accomplish anything like this. I'm one of them."

"I didn't start out with a job like you have," she said. "You have no idea how blessed you are. There are a lot of people who would do anything for the chance to drive around in a new car, calling on furniture stores."

"If my job is so wonderful, why am I so miserable and so broke?"

"It's one thing to work hard, and quite another to work smart. Do you really want to know how I did it, and how you can do it too?"

"Of course."

"Do you think you can trust an old woman?"

"What does that have to do with anything?" I asked.

"If I am going to help you, teach you, and loan you money, I have to know everything about your financial life. You will have to trust me, like you would a banker asking for financial information. Do you think you can do that?"

"You want financial statements, balance sheets, stuff like that?" I asked.

"And more."

"Like what?" I asked. She got up and went over to the desk. She returned with another savings register, but when she handed it to me, I could see this one was blank.

"Write your name on it," she said.

"Am I going to open a savings account?" I asked, hoping she had decided to make a deposit in my name.

"No," she said. "We can't determine how much you need until we know how much you have and how you are spending it. For the next thirty days, I want you to track your daily expenses and every other financial transaction by writing them down. If you spend a dollar for a Coke, write it down in this book. If you charge gas on your VISA, write it down. If you write a check, make a deposit or a withdrawal from the money machine, write it down. I want every financial transaction in your life written down in this little book."

"You're asking a lot," I complained. "I don't ever write anything in a register."

"Two or three minutes a day, at most," she shot back. "If you are not willing to do that, then there's nothing I can do to help you."

"I'll do it," I promised.

"Checkmate," she said, yawning while making her last move. It was time for me to leave.

"What about my house? I can't make the payment. You said you would loan me money. What about that?" I realized I was being pushy, but I was desperate.

"You won't lose your house in thirty days," she said. "It will take at least that long for you to master the discipline of tracking daily expenses."

"Then you will loan me the money?" I was determined to pin her down, get an answer, one way or the other.

"As I said earlier," she responded, thoughtfully, "I don't like throwing good money away. Until you learn the laws of financial success, you frankly are a bad credit risk."

"I suppose there are fifty laws," I said, starting to feel that I had gotten my hopes up for nothing.

"Altogether, I suppose there could be that many, perhaps more. But there are only four main laws," she said, beginning to rub her chin thoughtfully. There was a long silence as we looked into each other's eyes. I had no idea what was going on in her head, only that something serious was happening, and it would be best for me not to disturb the silence.

"I'll tell you what I'll do," she said, finally, her words slow and deliberate. "When you have demonstrated to me that you have mastered the four laws, I'll loan you all the money you want."

"I don't believe you," I said, emotion in my voice. I felt like I was going to cry. She had no right to toy with me like this.

"You don't trust me?" she asked.

"Get real," I said, starting to feel angry. "Remember the days when you were scrounging in the garbage bins? If a grocery clerk had offered to give you all the money you wanted, would you have believed him? Or would you have laughed at him?"

"I would have slapped him for being so cruel," she said.

10

"Now you know how I feel." Again there was a long pause as we looked into each other's eyes.

"I'll put it in writing," she said, turning and walking over to the desk. All I wanted to do was go home, but I waited in silence as she scribbled something on a piece of paper.

When she finally handed me the paper, I could hardly believe what I was reading.

To Whom It May Concern:

Being of sound mind, I, Mary Sessions, do hereby agree to loan money to my neighbor, Paul Smith, when he has demonstrated to my satisfaction that he has mastered the four laws of financial success. No collateral will be required for said loan. The interest rate will be 8%; the terms of payback will be negotiated at the time the loan is made, and the amount shall not exceed $2,000,000.

Mary Sessions

I was speechless. Carefully I folded up the paper and placed it in my pocket, along with the blank register. As I walked home, I had the strongest feeling that Mary Sessions was going to change my life. I was determined to do all she asked. I also decided I needed to impress her by winning the next chess game.

*The financial record-keeping functions essential to the success
and survival of any business are equally beneficial and
necessary in the financial lives of individuals
and families.*
—Blaine Harris

School Begins

After a few days of recording every financial transaction, I
dropped in on Mary one evening to show her my register and what I was doing. She was right. It took only a few
minutes a day, but I didn't like doing something that sometimes
seemed so trivial and tedious. She seemed pleased that I came
to see her, and wanted to play another game of chess, but I
said I didn't have time.

"But isn't it a little silly recording every donut, Coke, and
quarter for the parking meter?" I asked, attempting to express
my frustration.

She invited me to sit down beside her on one of the
sofas. Thoughtfully, she rubbed some of the aging spots on her
left hand.

"Tracking daily expenses is the first necessary step toward
any kind of financial success," she said. "A good business records
every financial transaction in basically the same way you are
doing it. Every penny coming in and every penny going out is

accounted for, in writing. From this raw data, the many reports for management, stockholders, and tax collectors are assembled.

"I had a friend who was an accountant for Ford Motor Company. He said the company had to present its financial information three different ways: one for management, one for stockholders, and one for the IRS. Without the raw data from every financial transaction, and the resulting reports and documents, no business can survive.

"You have to be able to count it or measure it if you want to manage it. How can you tell if you are winning or losing if you don't keep score? Doesn't it make sense that the financial principles absolutely essential for the success and survival of any business are of equal value in managing the finances of private individuals and families?"

"Yes," I said, and started to get up. She motioned for me to stay put.

"You see, businesses and wealthy people hire accountants and bookkeepers to track their money. Financially unhealthy people don't. That's one of the reasons they stay financially unhealthy. You think you are not wealthy enough to hire an accountant, so I am teaching you how to do it yourself.

"That which we focus on daily becomes easy or automatic. It's not that the nature of the task becomes easier, but your ability to handle it increases. In a tough game situation, a basketball player who will spend a few hours every day practicing shooting and fundamentals will find himself on automatic pilot, so he doesn't have to think about what he is doing. He doesn't have time to think. Finances are the same way. If you spend a little time every day doing fundamental stuff, like recording expenditures, you'll find yourself on automatic pilot and in control when the tough problems come along. Your ability to handle big financial problems increases as you expend daily effort on fundamentals."

As she talked, I had the feeling that she was telling me things I already knew—things buried in some deep, forgotten place. Her words were bringing truth to the surface.

School Begins

"Over the years, I've learned to keep my weight down," she continued. "It wasn't easy, but one of the strange phenomena of dieting is if you can discipline yourself to write down on a piece of paper the calorie count in every item of food you eat, and if you don't do anything else, you begin to lose weight. The process of counting calories alone will bring about weight loss. Isn't that interesting?"

"Are you trying to tell me that merely writing down my financial transactions will ease my financial problems?"

"Absolutely. You will find money that's been slipping through the cracks. Tracking helps you see the cracks so you can plug them up, so you can have more money for the important things."

"Good," I said, getting up to leave. "I'll keep tracking."

Again, she motioned for me to sit back down. "There's more."

"The best computer in the world is the one between your ears," she began. "Everyone has a personal computer more powerful than anything at the Pentagon, but most people don't give their internal computers a fair chance to help them, especially when it comes to finances." She reached forward, picked up one of the castles on the chessboard, and began playing with it.

"The computer in your head can't help with your finances if you don't give it the raw data to work with. And you can't second-guess your computer by giving it limited information. It doesn't play its best game with a partial deck. It has capabilities far beyond your conscious abilities. Don't limit its effectiveness by giving it partial or limited data. Give it everything. Give it the data from every financial transaction in your life, then stand back and let it go to work for you. You will be amazed at how much better you will be at solving your financial problems. Go home and track everything. Get your wife and children to do it too."

"Fat chance of that ever happening," I said. "They are a lot worse at managing money than I am."

"Next time you and Judy discuss the household budget, give her one of these little registers and ask her to record her transactions. If she prefers to log her transactions in her phone or in another way, that is fine. Just make sure you share why tracking is important. Tell her in a month you will add up the transactions together and decide if anything needs to be changed. Doing this together will help you become more unified as a couple and get you on the same page in building lasting, financial health.

"Do the same thing with the children and their $40 allowances, but tell them if they can only account for half of what you give them, when allowance time rolls around again, you will give them only half as much. Their monthly allowances will equal the total of the transactions in their registers, not to exceed the $40 received at the beginning of the month. Be tough, but not mean. They'll come around."

As I walked home that evening I was determined to become a tracking fanatic. I wrote down everything for a month. Judy and the children, with the expected protest, wrote down most things. I didn't show them the $2 million promissory note. That was my private secret, my private hope.

I began to make some interesting discoveries, like Judy and me running up between $85 and $100 a month in overdraft fees. That was as stupid as using $20 bills to test paper shredders. We put a stop to it.

I also discovered Judy and the children were ordering two or three movies on demand three or four nights a week in addition to an unused subscription to a premium channels option, costing us over $100 a month. Using the reasoning that the children needed to be doing better in school, Judy and I set the rule that on demand movies could be purchased on Friday or Saturday night only, unless special circumstances approved by Judy and me directed otherwise. We also cut the premiums channel down to basic. These adjustments saved another $75. By the end of the month, I had an extra $300 and was able to pay all the bills, but I was still a month behind on the house payment.

If you can't measure it, you can't manage it.
—George Odiorne

The First Law

Not only did I become addicted to tracking, recording in the little register every penny that passed in and out of my possession, but we all agreed that Judy and the children should keep doing it too so that we would have a true picture of what was happening in our household. Since a good portion of my income passed through their hands, it was essential for them to be involved. Of course, they were not as excited about the process as I was, and they couldn't understand why I was suddenly so determined to track every penny in our household. They still didn't know about the $2 million carrot Mary Sessions was dangling in front of my nose. I didn't want to use that to bring them around. I would tell them later. It would be a wonderful surprise.

The idea that fascinated me was Mary's claim that the process of tracking, by itself, would improve our financial situation—like counting calories helped keep her weight down.

The 4 Laws of Financial Prosperity

One night, while browsing through my library, I found a neat tracking story in a book titled The Game of Work, by Chuck Coonradt, in which Lee Nelson related how this tracking helped him in a teenage work experience. The following is the story in Lee's own words.

>*My first real contact with (tracking)…occurred one afternoon during my first after-school job as a bag boy at a Safeway grocery store in Walnut Creek, California, earning $1.33 an hour. It was probably the first or second day of my employment when the assistant manager took me into the back room and showed me three 4' x 8' plywood bins filled to overflowing with empty pop bottles.*
>
>*The assistant manager explained that the bottles needed to be sorted by kind into cases before they could be picked up by the various vendors. He explained why there were so many bottles in the bins, that the adult clerks hated to "work bottles," and avoided the task whenever possible. That was why I was being given the job—as a 16-year-old kid, I was at the bottom of the pecking order.*
>
>*The manager introduced me to the corner of the back room designated for sorting bottles. He showed me where the empty cases were stored; which bottles could be combined in the same cases, which had to be kept separate; and where the cases of empties needed to be stacked. Just when I thought I knew all there was to know about the new task and was ready to go to work, the manager said, "It takes most clerks one hour to do a bin. I hope you can do that well."*
>
>*He looked at his watch. I looked at mine.*
>
>*"Let me know when you've finished the first bin," he said, then added, "Some of the bottles have leftover pop; help yourself." He smiled at his sick attempt at humor, then turned and walked away.*
>
>*Suddenly, my work had meaning. Working the bottles was not just another job that needed to be done. A standard had been set by which my performance would be measured. My progress was*

being tracked. The manager was keeping score on my efforts. I was keeping score too. My palms began to sweat. I looked at the bins of bottles with new interest.

Comparing working bottles with my favorite sport, basketball, the manager had put me into a real game situation and turned on the scoreboard. In corporate terminology, he had ordered the accountants to track and report the progress in my department. I flew at the bottles.

An hour and ten minutes later, I finished the first bin, frustrated with my clumsiness, but confident that if I persisted, I could beat the magic 60-minute barrier—the accepted standard in my new working world.

I became the designated bottle worker in that store, delighting the clerks who hated this work. A record was kept on how long it took me to work each bin of bottles. After about a month, I worked three overflowing bins of bottles in one hour—three times the acceptable rate set by the clerks. The manager was pleased; the other workers talked about it.

I believed I was possibly the fastest bottle worker in the entire Safeway chain. I felt like I had accomplished something significant. Maybe the other workers knew more than me about checking, cutting meat, or trimming lettuce—but I knew more about working bottles and could do my job at least twice as fast as anyone else in the store. Because my performance had been measured and reported back, it had improved beyond anyone's expectations.

The manager of the night stocking crew heard about the kid with the fast hands and arranged for me to be promoted to the position of night stock clerk as soon as school was out. The night crew worked from 11 p.m. until 8 a.m., and my hourly wage was increased to $2.42 per hour.

The night manager had a competitive personality, on and off the job. Every task was a race to see who was best and fastest. At the end of a night's work, a typical comment was, "Big load coming in today. Better wear your runnin' shoes tonight."

When I arrived to begin work, he would say how many cases

arrived on the truck that afternoon. "Only 721 cases today. Ought to be through about 4:30." Then we'd go to work.

My eyes couldn't keep up with his price marker as it flew over the cans. He could throw six soup cans at a time onto the shelf, three in each hand, the labels all facing forward when the cans came to rest in perfect rows. As much as he loved speed, he never sacrificed quality. On Tuesday night, when we washed and waxed the floors, his mop could perform more tricks than a witch's broom. He had learned that in the Navy.

The night manager challenged me to try to keep up with him, an impossible task at first. But I tried very hard, and every week got a little closer. It seemed every task was timed and measured, even the tearing up of boxes for the incinerator. Speed and accuracy were the game, and we kept score. It made the work fun, like sports. I liked to go to work.

Some of the night-crew workers didn't like to compete with the manager and me. They thought we were too "gung ho." They seemed to prefer watching the clock instead of beating it.

It felt good to walk outside after a night's work, my body winding down after running to keep up with or beat the manager, then hear him throw down the challenge to come back that night with my running shoes. His words were music to my ears. I felt like an athlete getting ready for the big game.

Sometimes I think back on that first experience with the bottles, and wonder how things might have turned out if the manager had merely told me to go in the back room and work bottles until quitting time and had not tracked my progress.

Lee's story supports the universal truth that *when performance is measured, performance improves because you receive comparative feedback.* George Odiorne said, "If you can't measure it, you can't manage it."

One Wednesday night, Judy announced that because of some volunteer work she had been involved in, she had received four tickets to a figure-skating competition in the city on the upcoming Saturday night.

"What a strange coincidence," I said, explaining that at work that afternoon, my company had given four ice hockey tickets to each sales rep who reached his quota the previous month. The hockey game was Saturday night too, and it was just a few blocks from the figure-skating competition.

My son Billy and I wanted to go to the hockey game. Judy and our daughter wanted to go to the figure-skating competition.

"I can't understand why anyone would rather watch a bunch of guys fighting on the ice over the beauty and grace of figure skating," Judy argued.

"Hockey players are better athletes," Billy protested. "They skate circles around those figure skaters."

"They cannot," Lisa shot back. And so the discussion began, lasting an hour or more. I'm not sure who won. It just seemed refreshing to see the family doing something like this instead of watching television. The end result was that we decided to go to both events—the first part of the figure skating and the second half of the hockey game.

I enjoyed the figure skating more than I thought I would. Even Billy offered polite applause with everyone else when each skater, or pair of skaters, finished and when the judges held up the cards with the individual scores ranging from about 4.5 to 6.5. The skaters politely accepted the judges' evaluations, whether they were happy about the scores or not.

At one point, a pretty 16-year-old girl fell down during the last part of her routine. She started to cry. There were oohs and ahs in the audience as people felt sorry for the poor girl. After her performance, when one of the judges, a bald man in a white turtleneck sweater, held up a score card with 4.5 written on it, Billy was the only one who booed.

The hockey game was different. The first time a player fell hard on the ice, the crowd hardly noticed, except for Billy who made a few oohs and ahs, imitating the figure-skating crowd.

Then he brought our attention to the fact that the player on the ice had not begun to cry.

"Oh stop it," Lisa said.

Billy noticed other differences, like when an official made a particularly questionable call, the players complained and the fans booed. Some even threw things at the official.

Later, one of the players was put in the penalty box for tripping up the official that made the questionable call. There were two or three good fights during the match, and whenever the home team scored, the fans went wild. The players skated hard, and the fans were loud during the final period, with the home team behind by a single goal.

On the way home we had a lively discussion over the differences in the two ice-skating competitions we had witnessed. Both events involved skilled athletes who had spent many years preparing to perform.

I suggested that perhaps the reason the figure-skating crowd and performers were so polite was the fact that nobody knew the score until the performance was over, and it was too late to do anything about it. I pointed out that the reason the final period of the hockey match was so wild was because the home team was one goal behind. The players were skating harder to catch up, and the fans were cheering them on. I speculated that if a figure skater knew she was half a point down while she was performing, she would skate harder in an effort to catch up.

The fans at a figure-skating event don't know what is happening either. They don't know if a particular skater is falling behind, catching up, or not even in the running—so the applause is polite. When the judges finally hold up their score cards, the performance is over, and it is too late to do anything.

"With computer technology the way it is," Billy suggested, "they ought to develop a system where each judge has an electronic scoreboard above his head, and a dial with 1–10 numbering, so whichever number the judge turns to, that is the number on the scoreboard. All the boards read 5 when the performance begins, and the judges would turn their dials up or down as the performance develops. The fans and skaters would then know the score during the performance and could react accordingly. The fans, being able to see the changing numbers, would know whether or not to cheer or boo. The skater would become more aggressive in an effort to catch up, or more conservative in an effort to protect a comfortable lead."

Lisa pointed out that the girl cried when she fell down, not because the fall hurt, but because she knew the judges were lowering her score. "Hockey players would cry too," she added, "if the officials took a point off the scoreboard every time one of them fell down."

"They would not," Billy argued.

Suddenly, I saw an opportunity to tie all of this in with our family finances. "The big difference between figure skating and ice hockey is the scorekeeping," I said. "In figure skating, nobody knows the score until the performance is over, so the crowd is polite, and the performer is careful. When the judges finally hold up their cards, the results are so subjective, the high and low scores are thrown out. It's a bad system, but I guess it's all we have until someone like Billy comes up with something better."

"On the other hand," I continued, "in ice hockey the fans, the players, and the officials know the score at all times. The official can't change the score if a player hits him with a stick or if a fan throws a cup of beer at him. The play changes as a team aggressively tries to catch up or becomes more defensive in protecting a lead."

"It's more fun when everybody knows the score," Billy added.

"Exactly," I said. "That's why I have been trying to get all of us to keep score with our family finances. It's not fun to lose. Every month when I sit down to pay the bills and don't have enough money to pay them all, I realize we've lost again."

The 4 Laws of Financial Prosperity

I told them what Mary had promised, that if we would keep score on a daily basis by tracking all of our financial transactions, we would start winning the money game. I said I was determined to do that, and needed their help and cooperation.

Lisa asked if we could still afford the vacation to Yellowstone we had been talking about. I said we would still go on the vacation if we could pay for it with cash. I would not charge a vacation on a 20% VISA card. Furthermore, the first 10% of every paycheck was already committed to paying ourselves first, and that money at the present time was committed to getting rid of our debts. If we could find the vacation money in the remaining 90% of my income allocated to living expenses, then we could still do the vacation. Judy suggested we set up a special savings account for vacations. I agreed to do it.

I reminded them that as we persisted in tracking all of our expenses, we would discover expenses that were not as important as our family vacation. These expenses could be eliminated or reduced, and that's how we would find the money we needed. But everyone had to help.

As a parent, you always wonder if serious discussions like these sink in. But in the coming weeks, I realized an impact had been made. Billy bought a new pair of basketball shoes through an online discount shoe store for about half the price we had previously paid for the name-brand shoes. He insisted we put the difference in our vacation account. At prom time, Lisa borrowed a dress instead of buying a new one, on the condition we would put the dress money into the vacation account. As the end of school approached, we realized that even though the vacation might not happen until August, it was indeed going to take place without going further into debt.

Billy and I found ourselves in an ongoing discussion about tracking and scorekeeping in sports. We noticed the score is almost always the first thing the news reports about any sporting event. Everybody wants to know who won, by how much, and which players scored the most points. Every sport has scorecards, scoreboards, and stat sheets.

In sports, especially professional sports, measurements are continually added to increase player performance and fan interest in the game. Baseball has what they call the "slugging percentage" in addition to the batting average and runs batted in. In golf, they have driving-accuracy measurements, putting percentages, number of greens hit, and putts per round. Some basketball coaches are monitoring points per possession in an effort to measure the effectiveness of both offensive and defensive strategies. Good coaches understand that *when performance is measured, performance improves.*

We discussed how these principles apply to money. If you measure and track every dollar—if you keep score—you will play the game better and your win/loss percentage will go up.

One day I tried to explain all of this to a co-worker. He decided to go home and look over his bank statement and discovered the health insurance package he had canceled more than a year earlier was still activating the automatic monthly withdrawal. He thought he had canceled the policy with a phone call when he had started another policy. For over a year, he had been paying on both policies, wasting or throwing away over $2,000 in duplicate insurance fees. The first company wouldn't refund the money because they had no written record of a cancellation. *Had he been tracking his expenses on a regular basis, this would not have happened.*

In time, I realized good things were happening in my family. The children, especially, were learning to manage money, something they didn't seem to learn in school.

You can ask anyone which is most important—their family, or their job or business—and they will look at you funny as if wondering why you would ask a question where the answer is so obvious. Of course, the family is more important than the job or business.

The 4 Laws of Financial Prosperity

If the family is more important, then why don't we manage family finances with the same care, detail, and professionalism used in managing business finances? *If businesses ran their finances the way most families do, the business failure rate would skyrocket.*

What most of us don't seem to understand is that progress in our financial lives, not just sports and business, is directly related to the ability to measure. Four hundred years ago, the most portable mechanical timepiece was a water clock on a wagon. It was 10 feet high, weighed 300 pounds, and you had to pull it around with a horse. And it didn't keep good time if the water slopped around. The smallest unit of length measurement was the distance from King Henry's thumb to his nose, a yard. Everything they built was designed around that unit of measurement.

Today we are much better at measuring things. We have memory chips and integrated circuits. Our ability to measure and keep track of numbers is growing faster than anyone ever guessed. In the mid-1980s, Microsoft chief Bill Gates said, "640K ought to be enough for anyone." By the mid '90s, 640K computers were more obsolete than manual typewriters.

Thanks to computers, almost anyone on a daily basis can know how much interest they are paying or earning and exactly how much money they still owe on debts. It is even possible for private individuals with modest incomes to access instant, personal financial data online giving the exact status of financial goals, and a detailed accounting of spending for the month. Anyone can have a personal accounting and scorekeeping system.

One of the greatest rituals occurs at lunch when three or four friends get together to eat and enjoy each other's company.

"How are things going?" someone asks.

"Great, except I have a little bit of a cash-flow problem. Sure hope one of you picks up the tab today."

Everyone nods with solemn understanding. "Boy, we sure know what that's like. Why is it that everybody seems to have a cash flow problem?"

The First Law

What are these people talking about? Cash doesn't flow, not like water. Or does it? Water is a powerful resource. When left unrestrained, its flow can be very destructive. Money is also a powerful resource and, like water, when allowed to flow unrestrained, can be very destructive to households and families.

If you have a leaky faucet system in your kitchen sink, before you know it the small amount of water that drips out on a continual basis soon has wasted large quantities of water—and you weren't even aware of it. Likewise, if you have a leaky financial system in your household, great sums of money will be wasted and lost before you know it.

Money that is allowed to leak out on a continual basis with hardly a second thought jeopardizes the things in life that are of the greatest value to you. *A leaky financial system that allows cash to either drip, drizzle, or flow out untamed, sacrifices what you want most in life for the things you want right now.* These kinds of sacrifices rob individuals and families of the freedom and peace of mind that comes from directing money toward its greatest and most powerful use rather than being frivolously wasted through instant gratification spending.

Tracking enables us to identify the leaks or flow of where our money is going and redirect it to a much greater purpose. It's a simple principle, so why don't the majority of people do it? There are a dozen excuses—

"I'm too busy." "I don't want to know." "It's not important." "I don't have time."

And the list of excuses goes on. Now is the time to let go of the excuses. The reality is those who accumulate wealth, not just earn a lot of money, commit to knowing what is going on in their financial lives and track the patterns in their spending habits. The tracking process takes only a couple of minutes a day, yet frees up a tremendous amount of time from worrying and dealing with financial chaos.

Wise people look past the excuses and find the exact places where their cash flew when they thought it was going to flow.

The 4 Laws of Financial Prosperity

They backtrack along the cash pipeline looking for the leaks, knowing that if they can find the leaks, they can fix them.

You've got to measure it before you can manage it. Like in the bottle story at the beginning of this chapter, when performance is measured, it improves. When it is measured and reported back, the rate of improvement accelerates, a principle explained by Thomas Monson in a book many years ago.

Tracking—the first law of financial prosperity.

Personal goal setting is the strongest force in the world.
—Paul J. Meyer

The Second Law

Proudly, I made my report to Mary. As we began our second game of chess, I told her about the registered letter from the IRS at the post office, and how I was worried about being audited and having my personal business deductions disallowed because I didn't have receipts.

"Next year you won't have to worry about that," she said. "You'll have all your transactions recorded in these little books."

"But what do I do now?" I asked.

"Open it. It may not be as bad as you think." She began to laugh.

"What's so funny?" I asked.

"That you are so afraid of the IRS."

"If you were in my shoes, you would be afraid too."

"No I wouldn't."

"Why?"

"I used to be an IRS auditor."

"Really?" I asked, reaching for the register, thinking I had better be moving along. Suddenly, I felt very uncomfortable knowing I had been spilling out the secrets of my financial troubles to an IRS agent.

"Those nights I was fishing through the dumpsters, I was studying accounting," she explained. "When I got my degree, the IRS gave me a job. I became an auditor."

"People working for the IRS don't make enough money to live like this," I challenged. "They certainly don't make enough to make $2 million unsecured loans to neighbors."

"They do if they use their money wisely," she argued.

"What is that supposed to mean?"

"My job was to review tax returns. I saw the returns of the rich and the poor. I saw teachers earning less than $45,000 a year who were financially independent. I saw doctors earning $300,000 a year who were at the edge of bankruptcy. I was always amazed at how one person earning $60,000 a year could live so much better than another earning the same amount. Studying thousands of returns every year, I learned some valuable lessons.

"While auditing the records of very successful people, I made some good friends and learned some valuable lessons. I saw where smart people put their money and where other people squandered theirs.

"I built a $20 million net worth, not from my IRS paycheck, but from what I did with my savings from those paychecks. But that's enough for tonight. Open the registered letter. It may not be as bad as you think.

"Checkmate," she said, winning our second game of chess.

She was right. The letter informed me that I had made an error and owed them an additional $431. Mary told me to send them $75 with a note saying I would send them that amount every month until the debt was paid in full.

After two months of tracking my financial transactions, I went over to Mary's for a third game of chess. I told her I had called the leasing company and proposed I drive my car for another year if they would lower the payment amount and apply the difference to what I owed them for high mileage. They accepted my offer.

I told her tracking had helped a lot, and I was willing to continue doing it, but I still had too many money problems. I told her I was ready to learn the second law.

She said the second law was setting targets or goals.

"We have already talked about the computer between your ears," Mary began. "Through your tracking, you are putting a lot of financial information into your computer that it doesn't know how to process yet. It doesn't know what to look for. It doesn't know to what end you want this financial data manipulated.

"You have to give your computer targets or goals. Then it goes to work manipulating the data you input to help you achieve those goals."

"Then I set my goal to have $50 million in six months," I said.

"Don't mock me," she said as we seated ourselves on opposite sides of the chessboard.

"Then my goal is to beat you at chess," I said.

"That's about as likely as finding $50 million," she challenged as she moved the first pawn.

"They always talk about goal setting at our sales meetings," I explained. "I guess I never paid much attention or believed it to be anything more than a gimmick used by management to get salesmen to work harder for less money. I don't have any financial goals beyond putting out today's fires."

"How much do you pay a month in interest on all your debt?" she asked, after four or five moves.

"About $1,500 a month," I said, without having to think very hard. The tracking had made me much more aware of where my money was going.

"How would you like it if your employer gave you a $1,200 a month, after-tax raise?" she asked.

The 4 Laws of Financial Prosperity

"My financial worries would be gone. Fat chance that would ever happen," I complained.

"Then give it to yourself. You don't even have to tell your employer."

"I don't understand. Do you want me to steal or embezzle?"

"Of course not. Just get out of debt. Not paying $1,500 a month in interest is just like getting a $1,200 a month, after-tax raise. Why don't you do that for yourself?"

"I can give you about eight reasons," I said. "There's a house mortgage, a home equity loan, five charge cards, a checking account overdraft note, and a debt to a leasing company. My monthly payments barely cover the interest—let alone the principal. I'm going to have to go further in debt when I buy a new car. Then the kids will be going to college. I am resigned to being in debt the rest of my life. There's no other way."

"Would you like to be out of debt and have that extra $1,200 a month?" she asked.

"Certainly, who wouldn't want that?"

"Most people don't seem to care. Otherwise they would do something about it."

"Most people probably don't know what to do," I added.

"If I could show you how to get completely out of debt in less than half the time, without increasing your income and without paying any more toward reducing your debts than you are paying today, would you want to select being debt-free as one of your targets?"

"More than anything," I said, "but how is that possible when I can barely make my interest payments?"

"In order for you to understand how easy it would be for you to get out of debt, you need to understand the third law. But before we talk about that, we need to finish this discussion about targets or goals. Should we pick being debt-free as your first target?"

"Sure," I said. "I guess I'll just have to take your word that it's possible."

The Second Law

She walked over to her desk, picked up a piece of paper and a pen, and brought them back to me.

"Write down your first goal," she said.

"Why?" I asked. "You don't think I could forget something like getting out of debt?"

"A goal that is not written down is just a wish," she explained. I wrote down, on the paper, that I was going to be out of debt in less than five years.

"Every day you see things you want," she explained. "A fancy car, a Caribbean vacation, a bigger home, a beautiful race horse..."

"Wait a minute! I'm not into horses."

"It doesn't matter. No matter what you want, you have to help your internal computer set priorities among all the desires and wants you keep throwing at it," she continued. "You want it to know that getting out of debt is more important than getting a new set of golf clubs. You do this by writing down your high-priority targets, then reviewing them frequently, especially before you go to sleep at night and first thing in the morning. If you keep telling your computer that getting out of debt is your first and most important financial target, it will get the message and go to work manipulating all the financial data you are feeding it to help you get out of debt. Do you have any other financial goals?"

"No."

"You said something about your children going to college in a few years. Do you think establishing a fund to help them get a good education would be a good second goal?"

"Sure," I said. "But I don't know how I can do that. I'll just have to trust you." I wrote down something about having a college fund with $40,000 in it by the time my oldest child started college. I had no idea how this could ever happen.

"How about retirement money for you and Judy?" she asked.

"An extra $3,500 a month on top of Social Security would be nice," I said.

The 4 Laws of Financial Prosperity

"Nice?"

"Wonderful. We wouldn't have to worry about money, or be a burden on the children in our old age."

"Write it down," she said. I did it, then told her I didn't want more than these three goals to worry about. She told me to put the original target or goal sheet in my files after I had made two copies—one for my calendar and appointment book where it would be easy to look at during my travels, and one to put by my bed where I could look at it every night and morning. I agreed to do what she asked, thinking that setting targets wouldn't be any harder than tracking daily expenses. But I also knew that setting targets and achieving targets were two different things.

"So what's the third law?" I asked. "Or are you going to make me wait?"

"Checkmate," she said, catching me by surprise and winning our third chess match. Now that we were finished playing, she wanted me to go. She said she would tell me about the third law after I had a chance to study goals and goal-achieving techniques for a while. So that evening, using the internet, I began my study on the power of goal setting.

Many people do not have goals, or their goals are too trivial. Few people realize the power in setting a goal then developing a plan to achieve that goal.

In addition to winning the lottery or finding your name on the will of a rich uncle, the simplest way to become a millionaire is to save $250 a month, averaging 8.5% return per year, during your forty-year working career. If you do that, you'll have $1 million in cash the day you retire. If your household income is $4,200 per month, the $250 is just 6% of your income, less than half the amount saved by some international workers.

If you have a 401k with matching funds available at work, you can just about cut the $250 in half, or retire with $2 million.

But everybody doesn't want to be a millionaire. Some of us just want enough so we are not worrying about money all the time. We need enough to pay for our childrens' education, own a comfortable home, be out of debt, be able to retire when we choose to instead of when we have to, and have enough in a retirement fund so in our old age, we won't be a burden to our children. If you only want these things, you might as well set your sights on being a millionaire, because that's how much you will need to accomplish these goals. But you can still do it on $250 a month, unless you have fewer than 40 working years ahead of you. If so, you will have to save more so you can get there faster.

In the absence of clearly defined goals, we are forced to concentrate on activity and ultimately become enslaved by it. If the goals were taken out of basketball, a bunch of people would aimlessly be running up and down the floor dribbling a ball. Who would want to watch that? Who would want to do that? If the goalposts and end zones were taken off football fields, the Lombardi Trophy would go to the team with the nicest legs. If the goals were taken out of hockey, you'd have 12 guys on the ice fighting. Some people think that would improve the sport.

If the goals were absent in any sport, the most significant aspect of recreational pursuit would be removed—goal setting and striving. There is something inherent that makes us want to do something better, faster, higher, shorter, or longer to win. And when it comes to the accumulation and preservation of wealth, the same goal-setting principles apply.

So you say it's fun to score touchdowns and shoot baskets; but it isn't fun—in fact it's downright hard—to put $250 a month into an investment account. Nobody ever said goal striving was supposed to be easy. In fact, if it's too easy, it's not fun.

What would happen if the Dallas Cowboys showed up for a Super Bowl game and there were no opponent? Who would sit around for sixty minutes watching their star player score touchdowns if no one were trying to tackle him? How fun would it be to watch the best basketball player in the game shoot baskets if three guys weren't trying to stop him?

The 4 Laws of Financial Prosperity

There's a price to pay if you want to achieve significant financial goals. But if you think it's too hard and requires too much effort to build a $1 million nest egg, think how tough it will be if you remain on the interest-debt treadmill and have no pension when you retire. General George S. Patton said, "A pint of sweat today will save a gallon of blood tomorrow."

Scott Peck began his best-selling book, *The Road Less Traveled*, saying, "Life is difficult. This is a great truth, one of the greatest truths. It is a great truth because once we truly see this truth, we transcend it. Once we truly understand and accept it—then life is no longer difficult. Because once it is accepted, the fact that life is difficult no longer matters."

This book is not a get-rich-quick panacea, but a guide to spending money in such a way as to achieve worthy financial goals.

The following are some time-tested guidelines for setting and achieving worthwhile goals, from *The Game of Work* by Chuck Coonradt.

Goals must be written. Some people say they can remember their goals without writing them down, but if their spouse calls and asks them to stop at the store on the way home and pick up five things, they automatically reach for a piece of paper to write down the five items so they won't forget.

Goals not written down are wishes. Goals not written down are easily forgotten or changed. Written goals that are internalized, by regular review, become reality. Many people resist writing down goals. They must think the top NFL team creates its plays in the huddle. One of the main differences between professional and sandlot football is the amount of written documentation for achieving goals.

A good team doesn't just set goals to win or to be the best. Good goal programs are detailed and specific—yards per carry, number of offensive and defensive plays, plays per series, etc. Major goals are usually supported by a greater number of subtargets. Achieving subtargets helps you reach the final goal.

The Second Law

We need written goals in managing money. None of us would build a $500,000 home without a set of plans. What would you think if your builder said, "We don't need plans. I've got a pretty good idea what kind of house you want. Let's break ground in the morning."

But an income earner producing $50,000 a year for ten years, a total of $500,000, will spend every penny without a set of plans or priorities.

Then at the end of ten years, having nothing to show for his $500,000, he will wonder why his outcome is not as he had envisioned it. Had he simply plotted his priorities, his dream would have become a reality.

Goals must be your own. You no doubt have observed people who go through life giving the minimum daily requirement at work. Yet, when the whistle blows, they are off to coach a little-league team, play in a bowling league, build a mountain cabin—do something they enjoy. You've noticed the transformation, the new energy, the intelligence, the creativity, the increased endurance, and capacity for work they have when they are doing things that interest them.

Nobody can set your financial goals for you. If you are going to be doing all of the work to achieve your goals, they need to be your own personal goals, no one else's. Mary directed me in setting goals, but in the end, they were my goals, not hers.

Goals must be positive. Vince Lombardi said the objective of football is to win—fairly, squarely, and by the rules, but to win. The goal in sports is not to avoid a loss or defeat. How many times have you seen a PGA golfer going down the stretch suddenly change his game plan to see his lead slip away? He is beaten because he loses the momentum of his earlier positive attack.

Possibly the most common goal in America is to lose weight. Sometimes we feel it would be easier to cut off an arm than diet to lose 20 pounds. Instead of having a negative goal measured in pounds, it is better to set a positive goal to achieve an optimal weight and maintain that weight once achieved.

The 4 Laws of Financial Prosperity

One of the problems with losing weight is that we, more often than not, gain it back again and perhaps more. There are several reasons for this, including negative feelings and thoughts associated with taking off unwanted pounds. Negative goals are not pleasant to visualize, so the tendency is to avoid them, forget them. Do you want to be thinking about bankruptcy all the time if your financial goal is to avoid it? Does it sound fun to constantly think about budgeting, belt tightening, and deprivation? It is much more pleasant to visualize how content we will be when we have no debt, how much fun it will be to get a call from our stockbroker saying our $600,000 retirement account fund earned another $50,000 last year. Think how proud you will feel when you write out a check for $12,500 to cover the first year's tuition when your child gets accepted to college.

In basketball and football, they count the points you score, not the ones you miss. Financial goals should be that way too.

Goals must be measurable and specific. In sports, we demand numbers, sometimes two or three places to the right of the decimal point. The times of swimmers, speed skaters, and downhill skiers are all measured in thousandths of seconds, and in order to separate one athlete from the other, these exact measurements are essential.

Why, how much, and by when? If you can't measure it, how will you know when you achieve it? Even intangible goals need tangible indicators. If you have a goal to be more patient, count how many times you lose your temper with your children in a month. If the numbers drop, you know your patience is increasing. Don't say, "I am going to be a better salesperson next year." Instead, write down how many sales calls you are going to make.

If you put a hundred people in a room and ask them how many would like to be financially independent, all of the hands will go up. Then if you ask how many have a current financial statement listing all of their assets and liabilities, no more than ten hands will go up. It's hard to get where you want to be if you don't know where you are right now. A saying at IBM states, "You get better results from what you inspect than what you expect."

Now, if you ask how many in the group have projections of what they want their financial statement to look like in five, ten, fifteen, or twenty years, maybe one hand will go up, and that person will become your millionaire. It doesn't make any difference what his or her background is, how much money he or she has, or what his or her current income is. That individual has a plan, and with that plan, you cannot turn the person aside. Goals must answer the questions why, how much, and by when.

Goals must be stated in the most visible terms available. When goals are measured in real terms, everybody knows the score. It's harder to rationalize, fudge, and cheat. There's no monkey business. When the points are displayed on the scoreboard, everybody knows what is happening, who is ahead, and who is catching up or widening the lead.

Instead of setting a goal to become rich, set a goal to be completely out of debt by a specific time; have X dollars in your retirement account by a certain date; be able to pay cash for that new Dodge truck by a certain date; or be able to pay for that European vacation by the summer of a certain year.

Goals must contain a deadline. If you don't have a deadline, you don't have a goal. Goals must include how much and by when. The most exciting play in all sports occurs in the last two minutes of the half and before the end of the game.

Deadlines allow the student who has slept in all semester to stay up all night studying for the final exam. Because of deadlines in telethons, 40% of the money is raised in the last 20% of the time. One of Murphy's Laws states, "The first 10% of the work consumes 90% of the time allowed for the job. The second 90% requires 90% of the time too, and that's why jobs take twice as long to finish."

Deadlines are the foundation of commitment. Deadlines are the adrenaline boosters. Deadlines are the instigators of achievement and inventiveness. A person four years from retirement suddenly has a lot more motivation to save than a person forty years from retirement. Unfortunately, waiting until retirement is knocking at the door creates unnecessary stress and generally poor results. Instead, setting incremental financial deadlines along the path of saving for retirement creates short-term urgency and long-term results. A goals program without deadlines is merely a philosophical statement.

Goals must contain personality changes. If you want to achieve the goals you set, you must be willing to make personal changes in your life. Too frequently, poor people have poor ways, not just in managing their money, but in managing their lives.

Mary reminded me that I must be willing to change. She told me about a book by J. Paul Getty. The title was *Being Rich.* Not how to get rich, but be rich. He talked about responsibilities associated with having wealth and the personality traits necessary to develop and manage wealth. Paul Meyer said, "You must first set goals to become before you set goals to have."

Goals are the intangible characteristics that make winners who they are. You cannot become a great downhill skier if you are afraid of personal injury. You cannot live on 90% of your income if you are frantic to keep up with the Joneses.

If you take an average individual in an average job earning an average income, you can guess that person will never get ahead as long as things stay the same. But put that person in a traumatic situation, maybe a costly divorce or a major medical operation, and that person will rise to the occasion and generate an increased income; or fall back into old habits, giving up or looking to someone else or the government to meet the current obligations. We shouldn't wait for a life tragedy to make us change; we can use target setting and goal striving to change on our own. By setting and achieving personal targets, we can change by choice.

Goals work better if they contain benefits and rewards. A good idea in setting goals is to establish an arbitrary reward when the goal is accomplished. When selected debts are paid off, treat yourself and your family to a getaway paid for with money you have saved. When all the VISA cards are paid off, treat yourself and your spouse to a lobster dinner—but don't use the VISA card to pay for it. Wouldn't it be better to buy a new suit as a reward for paying off the home equity loan instead of buying one because somebody decided to put the suits on sale? Every time you and your spouse get through another month of living on 90% of your income, treat yourselves to dinner and a movie in the city.

Goals must be realistic and obtainable. A yard here, a yard there. Woody Hayes, one of the great legends in college football, is synonymous with "three yards and a cloud of dust." With that concept, Woody dominated Big 10 football for decades. The three-yards-and-a-cloud-of-dust attitude will get you closer to your financial goals than any instant accomplishments or get-rich-quick schemes.

Financial Goals

Identify your six most important goals.

__ Become debt-free.
__ Retire early with financial security.
__ Buy/pay off a home.
__ Establish an emergency fund.
__ Reduce financial stress.
__ Establish a fund to care for aging parents.
__ Gain control of finances.
__ Reduce taxes.
__ Own a business.
__ Have money for a dream vacation.
__ Own a better car, free and clear.
__ Be able to fund college educations for children.
__ Help children with down payments for first homes.
__ Own a farm or a mountain cabin.
__ Own a motor home.
__ Build a swimming pool and spa.
__ Other _____

In the space provided below, write down your financial goals in order of importance, including the amount of money needed to accomplish each goal by each target-completion date:

Goal	Amount	Target Date
1.		
2.		
3.		
4.		
5.		
6.		

The Second Law

Just remember that even though there may be things in life more important to you than financial goals—a lasting marriage, happy children, fulfilling careers, humanitarian service projects—your ability to function in the more important areas of life is greatly influenced by your financial stability. If financial worries are causing heart palpitations and high blood pressure, you are less likely to help your new neighbors unload the moving van. If you can't pay your phone bill, you are less likely to drop everything and drive to Alabama to help flood victims. How would you feel if the doctor said you needed to move your spouse to a milder climate, but you couldn't afford to quit your job without crippling yourself financially? Having financial order and control in your life lays a foundation that enables you to devote more time, energy, creativity, and money to family, hobbies, even community or humanitarian service.

Mary reminded me from time to time that what we were doing was not about the love of money, but the love of life; about a better life available to anyone willing to change spending habits in order to achieve worthy financial goals. The amount of time you spend worrying about money is in inverse proportion to how well you manage your money. If you don't like worrying about money, apply the principles in this book so you won't have to spend so much time fretting over financial problems.

When I had learned everything I could about targets, I returned to Mary for another game of chess, and instruction on the third law.

Targeting—the second law of financial prosperity.

That which each of us calls our "necessary expenses"
will always grow to equal our income unless we
protest to the contrary.
—George Clason

The Third Law

The next time I went to see Mary, I figured I knew everything there was to know about goals, and was ready for
the third law. As soon as she invited me in, I asked her to tell
me about the third law. Without responding immediately to
my question, she went to the kitchen and fixed each of us a
cold drink. As she returned to her place at the sofa, she had
that look in her eye like she was sizing me up again, trying to
decide how much I was ready to receive.

"In order for your goals to become reality, you need a
plan to follow in achieving them. You can't put a realistic plan
in place without understanding the third law, so I probably
shouldn't make you wait any longer."

"Good," I said, "I'm listening."

"You'll find the money to fund your goals by living on less
than you earn. The third law is to live on less than you earn
so you can have a surplus to get you out of debt and invest in
assets that appreciate."

The 4 Laws of Financial Prosperity

"With two teenagers and a busy wife, there is no surplus at my house," I said. "There is never anything left over at the end of the month. Even with all the tracking, I am barely able to pay my bills. I don't know how we could spend any less."

"The third law doesn't say you have to spend less, just spend differently. You pay yourself first instead of last. You don't wait until the end of the month to see if anything is left over for yourself. You pay yourself first, then make yourself live on what's left for the remainder of the month. The key to having a surplus for your financial goals is to pay yourself first and then live on what's left over."

"That doesn't sound easy."

"It can be, but who said life is supposed to be easy? No one, regardless of income, can be financially successful unless they live on less than they earn. The third law is absolutely essential. I call it trimming."

"I don't know if I can do it," I said.

"There's someone I want you to meet," she said. "Lucas," she called, turning her head toward the back of the house. A minute later, her gardener entered the room, a handsome young man, perhaps in his mid-twenties.

"Lucas," she said to him. "I know this request is somewhat personal, but would you be willing to show Paul your transaction log for the money you make working for me?"

"No problem," Lucas said. He pulled up a window on his phone and handed the phone to me.

There were lines of transactions, only deposits, that seemed to go on forever. Each transaction was recorded every week, with some weekly amounts being a little higher and some a little lower, but each was around $250. The account balance on the screen was just over $25,000. I handed the phone back to Lucas. Mary thanked him, congratulated him on his continued progress toward his goal, and excused him to return to work.

"Lucas also washes windows for businesses and homes throughout the area. That phone log is specifically the money

46

he deposits, after taxes and withholdings, for the work he does for me. He has earmarked this money to pay for the last two years of his college education."

"That's impressive, but he doesn't have a wife and two children," I said defensively.

"He has a wife and a young son, and you make many times what he does but haven't saved anything."

"How does he do it… why does he do it?" I asked.

"He is absolutely focused on completing his bachelor's degree without incurring any debt so he is better able to support himself and his family.

He will be financially independent because he is able to live on less than he earns. You must do the same, but it will be much easier for you."

"How much must I cut our living expenses?" I asked, still not sure it was even possible.

"All three of your financial goals are easily within reach if you can trim your living expenses to 90% of your income."

"I don't see how living on 90% of my income will get me out of debt in five years," I said.

She handed me another piece of paper and asked me to write down all of my debts, the interest I was being charged on each, the monthly payment, and the balance remaining. It wasn't long until I had the entire page filled with numbers. Then, on another piece of paper, she had me list the debts in order, starting with the one with the lowest balance.

She asked me how long it would take to pay off the smallest debt if I applied an extra $300 a month generated by our trimming. It was a VISA card, and I told her I would have it paid off in less than three months.

Then she asked how long after that it would take to pay off the next debt, another VISA card, if I added the extra $300 to the regular payment, plus the payment I had been making on the retired first debt.

"Two months," I said. We continued this process, eventually using up five sheets of paper. Each time a debt was paid off, we added its payment to the accelerated payment on the next debt. By the time we got to the last debt, the house mortgage, I was making nearly triple payments. If my calculations were correct, and I had to do a little guessing, all of my debts, including the house mortgage, would be paid off in four and a half years.

I went over the numbers a second time, thinking I must have made a mistake. I realized I had probably been too conservative the first time. If I followed this payment schedule, I would be out of debt in about four years. I could feel chills in the back of my neck and a tear pushing its way into my eye. It had never occurred to me that anything like this was even possible.

But the key was trimming, finding that extra $300 a month, and keeping the monthly payments at the same level, even after debts were eliminated. I still wasn't sure I could do it.

"Why don't you give me a debt-consolidation loan?" I asked. "Then it would be easier. I could use your money to pay off all our debt costing more than 8%."

"We have an agreement," she reminded me. "First you must demonstrate your ability to live the laws. Your tracking is coming along fine. You have written down some worthy targets. Now you have to trim your living expenses to 90% of your income. It is time for Paul Smith to become a little bit like Lucas. Remember, there is only one more law after you master trimming, then you will have access to $2 million."

After returning home, I stayed up until 2 a.m. poring over bills, and my tracking records. I was determined to find an extra $300 for my Debt Eliminator program, but I still didn't know where it would come from. I had already cut back the gym membership, extra dance lessons, and video game subscriptions and eliminated the overdraft charges.

The first big breakthrough came when I was looking at my

bank statement. The previous month, I had noticed and eliminated the overdraft charges. Now I discovered additional charges
for things like minimum balance and maintenance fees. Looking
at my wife's statements, I found similar charges. Together we
were paying about $50 a month for the convenience of two
checking accounts. Judy and I talked about it, and decided to
close one of the accounts. We decided to go without the additional checking account until we had enough savings to qualify
for the free checking services. By combining our accounts and
maintaining a minimum balance, we eliminated the extra fees
associated with our previous accounts.

We reduced our cable television service level. Judy decided
she could do her own nails, and she started cutting Billy's hair.
Mine too.

Looking at the itemized charges on our cell phone bill, I
realized there were other services we could switch to that would
save us close to $40 a month without losing any of the features
or coverage that we currently had. I also learned that if I quit
continually updating to the latest cell phone model, it would
equate to a savings of around $50 each month.

In going over the internet bill and researching the internet
service options, I discovered that we were paying for an old
plan that provided slower than average internet connectivity
speed. We could bundle our internet and phone services and
save another $30 each month, plus make everyone happier with
faster service.

Catching the spirit of what we were doing, Judy offered to
wash my shirts and her blouses instead of sending them to the
laundry if I would do the dinner dishes three nights a week. I
agreed.

I turned the water heater down from 160 degrees to 140.
The gas company said that would save us at least $10 a month.
Billy and Lisa agreed to buy discount clothes when I told them
I was working on a program to pay their college tuition.

The 4 Laws of Financial Prosperity

We cleaned out the basement and donated $3,000 worth of items to Goodwill, a deduction that would save about $800 at tax time, or about $60 a month for a year. I didn't replace the chopped-up Christmas tree.

With the arrival of good weather, instead of going out to dinner every week, Judy and I started going on picnics. It was less expensive than going to restaurants, and a lot more romantic. We saved about $80 a month.

Once I got everyone tracking, I was shocked with how much we were spending for lunches, and most of it was on fast food. Just by becoming aware of the habit we had fallen into, mostly one that I had fallen into, we realized we could cut our lunch expense in half. To accomplish our goal, I committed to eat lunches I made at home when I was working in town; and when I was on the road, I stopped "super-sizing" every meal and would often eat fruit, carrots, and crackers for lunch instead of fast food. This change in habits would make me more conscientious about what I spent as well as about what I ate, improving my financial and physical health.

A nice side benefit I realized in the first two months was losing about 10 pounds. I felt so good I started jogging—our household finances and my health improved at the same time. Through this process, I learned that as I began implementing simple yet powerful financial changes into my life, the benefits spilled over into many other areas for me and for my family.

The key to living on less than you earn is to pay yourself first, as soon as you get your paycheck, and then live on what's left over. Those who wait until the end of the month to see if anything is left over before paying themselves never have any extra money for their financial goals. By default, they are helping fund everyone else's retirement rather than funding their own.

Everyone should ask, "Who are the most important people in my life?" If it's you and your loved ones, then maybe it's time to take a hard look at a spending program that is keeping the stockholders at the credit card company and Eddie Bauer happy, but is doing nothing to get you and your family any closer to your financial goals.

During the early part of your financial program, when you are paying off debts, it may not seem that you are paying yourself first. After all, the excess money is going to creditors, and you will never see it again.

You must look at accelerated debt payments as a process to prevent future interest burdens. If you pay off a $250,000 house mortgage in 15 years instead of 30, you will save $130,000 in interest payments, assuming a 5% mortgage rate. You must also realize it doesn't make economic sense to put your money into a 1% or 2% certificate of deposit when you are paying the equivalent of 25% interest on outstanding credit card balances.

As a general rule, the interest you pay when you are in debt is higher than the interest you will earn when you are out of debt and investing money. However, do not forget that the excitement, motivation, and discipline to achieve comes from eliminating debt while forming the savings habit—these two principles combined produce the most powerful way to pay yourself first.

After you make the decision to pay yourself first, the next step is to stop buying things you can't pay for with cash. Use a credit card for convenience only, not to bury yourself further in debt purchasing things that do not support your commitment to financial prosperity. Discipline yourself by paying the credit card off each month before incurring finance charges. If the balance is not paid off at the end of the month, cut up the card or at least put it away where it is not readily available to use until the balance is paid in full.

Some people have a hard time understanding that trimming is not an end to spending, but redirecting the way you spend. In applying the four laws, you become a power spender, trimming excess waste and realizing the most efficient use of your money in achieving financial goals. Trimming is exciting! It's really redirecting spending in order to accelerate your rate of progress.

Once a person has initiated a tracking process so every dollar is accounted for, set his or her financial goals, and trimmed away the fat in an effort to redirect those dollars toward achieving appropriate financial goals, then that person usually becomes more motivated than ever to increase earnings. The individual realizes, "Hey, if I had another $300 a month coming in, I would be out of debt in half the time. I would be a millionaire by age fifty-five and could retire ten years early.

Wow! Where can I find another $300 a month? But if I could figure out a way to earn another $600 a month..."

When first confronted with the challenge of finding additional money to fund financial goals, most people think the money simply isn't there. We can't take lunch money from the kids or gas money from Dad. We can't sell the house in the suburbs and move into an apartment in the city. We don't want to give the dog away so we won't have to buy any more dog food.

What people don't realize is that the simple process of tracking expenses, as discussed in this book, will help them find extra money they didn't even know existed—like the man who discovered he was paying premiums on two health insurance policies. He found an extra $250 a month without having to give up anything. What about the small-business owner who started tracking every dollar only to discover at tax time he had an extra $3,750 in deductions? If he's in the 30% tax bracket, those additional deductions saved him a thousand dollars, almost a hundred a month. Still, nobody has had to do any belt-tightening.

And who says belt-tightening is always bad? Suppose an individual, after a few months of detailed tracking, discovers he and his wife are spending nearly a $125 a month on fountain drinks and another $125 on alcoholic beverages. Neither one had any idea they were spending and consuming so much. They are faced with the hard truth that maybe they won't even be around to enjoy retirement if they continue filling their bodies with so much sugar, carbonation, and alcohol. Strictly for health reasons, they decide to cut these expenses down to $50 a month, and bingo, they have an extra $200 a month, almost enough by itself to fund their retirement program.

Then there's the busy couple like Judy and me, who are concerned about the below-average report cards of their two teenage children. While tracking family expenses, they realize they are spending $200 a month on an all-inclusive cable television package and periodic DVD rentals, and neither one of the parents watches more than three or four hours of television a month. Perhaps if this expense were eliminated, or drastically reduced to about $75 a month, it would be easier to get the children to read and do homework. How much would that $125 a month become in ten years if it were invested at 8% in a college education fund for the children? It would be $22,868. The children might call such a cut severe belt-tightening, unnecessary deprivation, or downright child abuse, but think how happy they will be when it comes time for them to pay for tuition, not to mention how much more prepared they will be for having traded some television time for some study time.

Present value tables are a wonderful motivation when you start to trim. These tables tell you what the $5 you saved by bringing your lunch to work will be worth when you retire. If you decide to buy $2,000 worth of mutual funds instead of a snowmobile, these tables will tell you how much it will appreciate by the time your children start college or when you retire. The table on the following page shows how different amounts of money invested monthly at 10% by people of various ages will grow over time into $1 million to $3 million nest eggs.

Once your tracking program is in place, the first and obvious trimming is getting rid of the waste and unwanted spending, like some of the items mentioned earlier. Then you take a hard look at your goals—where you want to be and where you are

The 4 Laws of Financial Prosperity

Save to Become a Millionaire★

Starting Age	Years Age 70	$1 Million	$2 Million	$3 Million
10	60	$21	$42	$63
15	55	$35	$70	$105
20	50	$58	$115	$172
25	45	$95	$190	$284
30	40	$157	$314	$471
35	35	$262	$523	$784
40	30	$439	$878	$1,317
45	25	$748	$1,495	$2,243
50	20	$1,306	$2,612	$3,918
55	15	$2,393	$4,786	$7,179
60	10	$4,842	$9,683	$14,525

★Approximate monthly amount to be invested at 10% to produce $1–3 million by age 70. Historically since 1920, the market has averaged about 10%.

now. You measure your current net worth (assets less liabilities) and subtract that amount from the net worth you would like to achieve, possibly at retirement. Divide this amount by the number of years until retirement, and you have a pretty good idea how much trimming you are going to have to do. Keep in mind that as you get closer to your goal, your assets are not only appreciating, but are producing income to buy additional assets, a process called compounding. In other words, once you get out of debt and start earning interest, time becomes your friend. A 25-year-old who bites the bullet and saves $500 a month until he is thirty-five, then decides he is tired of saving and never puts away another nickel the rest of his life, if he never spends the money he saved and it continues to compound at 8% per year, at age sixty-five he will have $1,000,324.

On the other hand, if a 55-year-old worker who has never saved anything decides to get serious about retirement and starts saving $500 a month, which he invests at 8%, ten years later at 65 he will have $91,473.

Both of the above people saved $500 a month for ten years. Both earned an average annual increase of 8% on their savings.

The Third Law

Yet the young person earned $908,851 more than the older person. The difference is time. The sooner you start on a savings and investment program, the better. It is better to save now and play later, than to play now and save later. Time is money, and the sooner you get it working for you, the better.

If you are already 50 or 55, don't assume it's too late for you to take control of your finances. If you start putting $500 a month into an 8% mutual fund at age fifty, you will have $295,510 when you retire at age 70. That's a lot more than if you didn't start saving at all.

In addition, people who are in control of their money have the capacity to be more charitable. If it were not for charitable people and charitable attitudes, our churches, museums, art centers, hospitals, schools, and society in general would suffer. Charitable people have trimmed unnecessary expenses and redirected them to greater priorities, which affords them the privilege of donating to worthy causes. True financial success requires proper financial balance.

The key to any kind of financial success is learning to live on less than you earn, thereby creating a surplus to invest in assets that earn interest or increase in value. Trimming is the process by which we do this. But no matter how good we are at trimming, it never seems to work if we wait until the end of the month to see how much is left over to invest. Pay yourself first, not last. As soon as you get your paycheck, take the 5%, 10%, or 15% you have identified as surplus to reduce debt and buy investments, and take that out first, forcing yourself to live on what's left over.

Most people who do this say they hardly notice any difference in their lifestyle. The tracking process alone can usually uncover enough inefficient spending and downright waste to more than cover a 10% debt elimination and savings program.

Most Americans, if they start early enough, can achieve financial security on a 10% savings program. If their goals are more aggressive, or if they don't start until later in life, 10% will not be enough. But before you determine how much surplus you have to create, you must first figure out where you are, where you want to be, and how many years you have to get there. These numbers will give you a pretty good idea where you have to start.

At first, I didn't believe Mary when she told me that after trimming my living expenses to the 90% level, I wouldn't miss that extra 10%. She said I might even want to start saving more than that—maybe 15% or 20%. She said if I would sit down and figure out how much quicker my financial goals could be realized with that increased payment, the idea of trimming living expenses even more would be very attractive.

She said it is important that you look at the amount you are saving not as a sacrifice, but as a payment to yourself to help achieve your most desired financial goals. The third law is about paying yourself first and then living on what's left over.

Trimming—the third law of financial prosperity.

The only thing worse than investing in things that depreciate
is paying interest on money invested in things that depreciate.
—Blaine Harris

Debt-Free

The next time I visited Mary, I had high hopes of learning the fourth and final law. But as we sat down for what I thought was our final game of chess, she wanted to talk about something else. Debt.

"Have you ever wondered why most American families who earn as much as you do seem to be struggling financially, when most of the families of the world live on less than $800 a month?" she asked. I didn't say anything.

"You nod with understanding when you see the financial struggle of a factory worker earning $10 an hour," she continued, "but you shake your head in amazement when a medical doctor with a guaranteed six-figure income declares bankruptcy. Regardless of income, most people are broke—just at a different level.

"There was a time in this country when the person who spent all of his or her income without saving anything was considered foolish," she added. "Today the person who spends all that he earns is only less foolish than the millions who spend more than they earn—thanks to easy credit. Why is it that the people in one of the richest nations in the world feel the poorest?"

"I don't know," I responded.

"Because they don't know how to manage their money."

She went on to explain that not only do we earn more than most of our world neighbors, but we worry more too. Worrying about money lowers the quality of life and causes health problems. In addition, 89% of divorces are attributed to financial mismanagement.

Part of the problem is the quality and quantity of advertising to which we are exposed. Every day we are bombarded with advertisements for home equity loans. There isn't a day that goes by without being encouraged to consolidate debts using the ever-so-precious equity in our home. "We'll help you get the money out of your house so you can use it on things you just can't live without."

Every day we get mailers offering new credit cards, some where our credit acceptance is guaranteed. Our children start getting these mailers when they are seniors in high school from companies trying to lure them into the interest trap before they know better.

Every one of these ads, just like every cigarette pack, should carry a warning that consumer debt is dangerous to your health, your marriage, and the overall quality of your life. The home equity ads convey the feeling that consumer debt is a warm, fuzzy blanket that will make you feel better and give you peace of mind. Nothing could be further from the truth.

Long after the thrill of the purchase has passed, the financial burden continues to linger endlessly and negatively affects all aspects of life. It should be obvious that if we continue to borrow the equity out of our home to pay for yesterday's meals and worn-out shoes, we've sacrificed what's most important in life for what we wanted at the moment. No home equity loan should ever be granted until after we have modified our spending habits that created the need for the loan in the first place.

Debt-Free

The first step toward financial peace of mind, if you are sick and tired of that trapped feeling, is to make the decision to do something, to take the no-debt pledge. I told Mary I had done that.

Mary said you must set your standard of living lower than your level of income, while many of your neighbors and friends set their standard of living at the limit of their credit-worthiness.

Mary said she knew a Vietnamese couple who lived on 20% of their income while saving up to buy their first restaurant. Most of us can get out of debt and achieve financial security by learning to live on 90% of our income.

Once you start living on less than you earn, you use the excess, or the amount you pay to yourself, to accelerate debt payments and to build wealth.

If you don't like living on less than you earn, and you don't want to give up the vacation home in Phoenix, then you ought to seriously look at options for increasing your income.

You can literally spend your way to wealth. Some people falsely associate the word *spend* with "waste" or "squander." To spend is to allocate. We all have resources that need to be allocated—like time and money. How we manage the allocation of these resources greatly impacts the quality of our future.

Even though we must learn to live on less than we earn, we still spend all that we earn. With a good financial plan, we don't spend less, we spend differently. We direct our money into channels that get us out of debt and build financial security. Instead of spending our way into a deeper and deeper hole, we spend our way to happiness and security. Other people do it, and so can we.

Mary said most people could get completely out of debt in about half the time without paying more each month than they are paying today on monthly debt payments. Many people don't believe this is possible, but it is true nonetheless.

The 4 Laws of Financial Prosperity

The following is a case study of John and Jill Sample, who planned to have their $31,131 in consumer debt paid off in six years, making regular payments that included $8,284 in interest. While using the Debt Eliminator program outlined at the end of this chapter, they were able to pay off their debts in three years and two months, paying $6,888 in interest. By adding another $100 a month, they could have been out of debt in two years and ten months and saved another $700 in interest.

The key to making the Debt Eliminator program work is to keep the dollar amount of monthly payments at the same level as debts are retired. For example, when the Samples' dentist was paid off, they took the $30 a month they had been sending to the dentist and applied it to the next targeted debt, thus accelerating its pay-down time.

Let's assume that after paying off all their debts, using the $100 accelerator, the Samples continued making the same payment into an 8% investment fund. By the time six years pass— the time they originally targeted to get out of debt—instead of just being out of debt, they have $49,251 in their investment fund. In other words, by using the principles taught in this book, in six short years, the Samples went from $31,131 in the red to $49,251 in the black, an $80,382 improvement in their financial net worth!

The first chart gives a breakdown of each of the Samples' debts including balances owed, interest rates, monthly minimum payments, number of payments remaining, and real debt, which is the sum of the remaining payments including principal and interest. The first chart also shows how long it will take the Samples to get out of debt on their current course, on the Debt Eliminator program, or on the Debt Eliminator program plus $100, and how the Debt Eliminator program plus $100 not only pays off the debts, but gives them $49,251 in savings at the end of six years.

DEBT ELIMINATOR

Prepared for

John and Jill Sample

	Principal Balance	Interest Paid	Investment Accumulation	Duration of Time

	Principal Balance	Interest Paid	Investment Accumulation	Duration of Time
Current Course	$ 31,131	$ 8,284	$ 0	6 Yr 0 Mo
Eliminator	$ 31,131	$ 6,888	$ 0	3 Yr 2 Mo
Eliminator* payment of $100	$ 31,131	$ 6,175	$ 0	2 Yr 10 Mo
Eliminator payment of $100	$ 31,131	$ 6,175	$ 49,251**	6 Yr. 0 Mo

Description	Interest Rate	Amount Left	Minimum Payment	Payments Left	Real Debt
Dentist	18.00%	485.00	30.00	19	560
Auto I	7.50%	3,325.00	190.0	19	3,532
Auto II	9.00%	8,800.00	310.00	33	9,932
Home Equity Loan	11.00%	12,000.00	320.00	47	14,772
Discover Card	19.50%	1,700.00	49.00	52	2,522
MasterCard	21.00%	1,985.00	53.00	62	3,255
VISA	19.80%	2,836.00	68.00	72	4,842
Total		31,131.00	1,020.00		39,415

*Based on total monthly payments of $1,120.00 ($1,020.00 current payment + $100.00 accelerator).

**Based on an 8% annualized return on investments.

The 4 Laws of Financial Prosperity

The second chart gives a month-by-month breakdown showing how each debt is systematically eliminated in thirty-four months using the $100 accelerator. The formula is quite simple. In the month following payoff of the first debt, the Samples add the amount of that payment to the payment on the second debt. When the second debt is paid off, they add the combined payments they have been making on the two retired debts to the payments on the third debt until it is paid off. They continue the process, keeping the combined total of all payments at $1,120 a month until all the debts are paid off in Month 34. This is called debt-payment compounding.

DEBT ELIMINATOR
Monthly Payments Required to Meet Your Target

Month Total	Dentist	Auto I	Auto II	Home Equity Loan	Discover Card	MasterCard	VISA	
Aug 20xx	130.00	190.00	310.00	320.00	49.00	53.00	68.00	1,120.00
Sept 20xx	130.00	190.00	310.00	320.00	49.00	53.00	68.00	1,120.00
Oct 20xx	130.00	190.00	310.00	320.00	49.00	53.00	68.00	1,120.00
Nov 20xx	112.94	207.06	310.00	320.00	49.00	53.00	68.00	1,120.00
Dec 20xx		320.00	310.00	320.00	49.00	53.00	68.00	1,120.00
Jan 20xx		320.00	310.00	320.00	49.00	53.00	68.00	1,120.00
Feb 20xx		320.00	310.00	320.00	49.00	53.00	68.00	1,120.00
Mar 20xx		320.00	310.00	320.00	49.00	53.00	68.00	1,120.00
Apr 20xx		320.00	310.00	320.00	49.00	53.00	68.00	1,120.00
May 20xx		320.00	310.00	320.00	49.00	53.00	68.00	1,120.00
Jun 20xx		320.00	310.00	320.00	49.00	53.00	68.00	1,120.00
Jul 20xx		320.00	310.00	320.00	49.00	53.00	68.00	1,120.00
Aug 20xx		143.02	486.98	320.00	49.00	53.00	68.00	1,120.00
Sep 20xx			630.00	320.00	49.00	53.00	68.00	1,120.00
Oct 20xx			630.00	320.00	49.00	53.00	68.00	1,120.00
Nov 20xx			630.00	320.00	49.00	53.00	68.00	1,120.00
Dec 20xx			630.00	320.00	49.00	53.00	68.00	1,120.00
Jan 20xx			630.00	320.00	49.00	53.00	68.00	1,120.00
Feb 20xx			310.00	320.00	49.00	53.00	68.00	1,120.00
Mar 20xx			310.00	320.00	49.00	53.00	68.00	1,120.00
Apr 20xx			310.00	320.00	49.00	53.00	68.00	1,120.00
May 20xx			460.14	489.86	49.00	53.00	68.00	1,120.00
Jun 20xx				950.00	49.00	53.00	68.00	1,120.00
Jul 20xx				950.00	49.00	53.00	68.00	1,120.00
Aug 20xx				950.00	49.00	53.00	68.00	1,120.00
Sep 20xx				950.00	49.00	53.00	68.00	1,120.00
Oct 20xx				950.00	49.00	53.00	68.00	1,120.00
Nov 20xx				950.00	49.00	53.00	68.00	1,120.00
Dec 20xx				950.00	49.00	53.00	68.00	1,120.00
Jan 20xx				348.91	650.09	53.00	68.00	1,120.00
Feb 20xx					285.47	766.53	68.00	1,120.00
Mar 20xx						537.43	582.57	1,120.00
Apr 20xx							1,120.00	1,120.00
May 20xx							346.22	346.22

Debt-Free

Before the Samples started the Debt Eliminator program, they were targeted to be out of debt in six years, or seventy-two months. When their debts were paid off in the thirty-fourth month, if they continue paying the $1,120 a month for thirty-eight months to the end of the original six-year period into an 8% growth fund, the compounded value of those payments at the end of the six-year period is $49,251.

Now, if you really want to get excited about what the Debt Eliminator program can do for you, make a list of your own debts on the Debt Eliminator Worksheet found in the Appendix. You'll need to know payment amounts, number of payments remaining, interest rates, and approximate balances. Fill in the blanks the best you can. If necessary, call financial institutions for additional information.

Once all the appropriate debt information is recorded in the first table, go to the left-hand column of the graph in the Appendix and enter the month and year for sixty consecutive months, starting with the current month. Now, moving horizontally across the top of the graph, write a name to describe each debt (VISA, pickup, home equity, etc.).

Be sure to rank the debts according to the number of payments remaining, starting with the one with the fewest remaining payments, not the one with the highest interest rate. The reason for this is to get into a situation where you are making double, triple, and quadruple payments as soon as possible. This gives you the feeling you are exterminating your debts with reckless abandon, a wonderful experience after years of feeling enslaved by them.

To determine the monthly payment total in the right-hand column, just add up all payments on the debts you listed and add the $100 accelerator. Don't worry about where the extra $100 will come from. Remember, the monthly payment amount in the right-hand column must remain the same as the debts are eliminated.

The 4 Laws of Financial Prosperity

Now, start filling in the columns, one row at a time, from left to right. If you listed the debts in the right order, the debt in the left column will be retired first. When you fill in the next row, take the amount you had been paying on the retired debt, and add it to the payment on the second debt.

At this point, you need to do a little creative arithmetic. Because you have increased the amount of the second payment, you have shortened the payoff time. Divide the new payment into the approximate balance, plus some estimated interest to determine how many months it will take to retire that debt. Continue filling in all the blanks, a row at a time, until the second debt is retired. Then add this payment to the payment of the third debt. Continue this process until all of the debts are eliminated.

Most people, when they are finished filling in the blanks, think they have made a mistake, because the amount of time required to get out of debt is much shorter than they first guessed.

Now, if you want to get more excited, look at the annuity table below and figure what your monthly payment amount from the right-hand column of the worksheet will be worth in five, ten, fifteen, twenty and twenty-five years, if you pay that amount into a 8% investment fund after all your debts are paid off. See how wonderful it is to have interest working for you instead of against you?

	$500	$600	$700	$800	$900	$1,000	$1,100
5 yrs.	36,738	44,086	51,434	58,781	66,129	73,477	80,825
10 yrs.	91,473	109,768	128,062	146,357	164,651	182,946	201,241
15 yrs.	173,019	207,623	242,227	276,831	311,434	346,038	380,642
20 yrs.	294,510	353,412	412,314	471,216	530,118	589,020	647,922
25 yrs.	475,513	570,616	662,718	760,821	855,924	951,026	1,046,129

Monthly Investment Annuity Table at 8%

*The people who understand money spend it on assets that
generate wealth. Those who don't understand money
spend it on things that consume wealth, and thus
the rich get richer and the poor get poorer.*
—Blaine Harris

The Fourth Law

The next time I saw Mary, I had been tracking my expenses
for three months and living on less than 90% of my
income for two months. I read my goal sheet every night and
morning, and three of my five credit cards and the overdraft
debt were gone forever.

When I explained all this to Mary, she said I was ready for
the fourth law.

"Once you get out of debt," she began, "You don't just
squander all that new money you will have by not having to pay
interest. You start buying things that appreciate in value. You
never stop spending; you just spend differently, more wisely.
You have to change. You need to become more interested in
mutual funds than convertible sports cars from Italy. We live in a
world of money, but managing money can be as complicated and
sophisticated as you want to make it. There's much to learn."

"So what is the fourth law?" I asked, wanting her to say it
in a few words.

The 4 Laws of Financial Prosperity

"First, let's play a little chess," she suggested. I followed her to the chessboard. As eager as I was to learn the fourth law, I was more eager to play chess. She had whipped me three times in a row. I was determined to engineer a different outcome this time.

She seemed intent on philosophizing on the fourth law. Good. I encouraged her to talk about that while I concentrated on winning the game.

"Albert Einstein once said one of the most powerful forces in the universe was compound interest," she said.

"Was that before or after he came up with the theory that laid the foundation for the invention of the atomic bomb?" I asked. "What do you think he meant?"

"It means a 15-year-old who can start investing $35 a month, and sticks with it, earning an 8% return, can reach retirement with an additional three quarters of a million dollars rather than the $35 a month just slipping through the cracks," she said emphatically. "It means a young single mother who prepares a few cheap meals a month so she can salt away $50 in a growth mutual fund, if she sticks with it, can accumulate a million dollars. It means Paul Smith can retire with a million dollars if he can live on 90% of what he earns, and invest the difference wisely."

"So what's the fourth law?" I asked, still concentrating on the game.

"About forty years ago," she continued, ignoring my question, "after I had mastered the first three laws, and had saved a little money to invest, I thought I'd make a killing investing in pork belly futures. I guess I was short on patience, but I was still tracking and trimming. I wanted to make a lot of money fast. Instead, I lost the entire $2,000 I had worked so hard to save. I was devastated. It was like I had lost all the money in the world. I thought I was going to have to take a second job to cover my losses."

The Fourth Law

"So what did you do?"

"I just continued tracking and trimming, but this time I did something different. As I was building a new nest egg, I started reading investment books and attending seminars. I wasn't about to lose $2,000 that fast a second time. And I didn't. Today my investments earn me over $2,000 a day..."

"Wow," I said, not meaning to interrupt her. But the thought of someone earning $2,000 a day while puttering in the yard and playing chess couldn't help but trigger a verbal reaction from me.

"I look at that $2,000 loss as the price I had to pay to learn the fourth law, or my tuition," she said. "If you listen closely to what I am saying, you can learn the fourth law for free."

"So what's the fourth law?" I demanded.

"I want you to attend a real estate seminar, and have a real estate professional show you at least one piece of property a week."

"All my money is committed to getting out of debt," I said. "I can't think about buying real estate."

"Nobody said anything about buying, at least not yet. I also want you to attend a stock, bond, and securities investment seminar, and read at least two books on the subject."

"I don't have any money to invest in stocks either," I said.

"But you will, so you must get ready now. I want you to read *The Wall Street Journal* and *Money* magazine, subscribe to an investment newsletter, and find a counselor or money manager who is more interested in a long-term relationship than short-term commissions."

"What is the fourth law?" I asked, thinking if I could stay on this track ten more minutes, I might win the game.

"Success happens when preparation meets opportunity. If you don't prepare, you will never be able to seize those wonderful investment opportunities that present themselves every day in the stock market and the world of real estate."

The 4 Laws of Financial Prosperity

"So the fourth law is preparation?" I asked, thinking I was about three moves from checkmate.

"I call it training, because training is the process of increasing your knowledge on financial topics while continually training, or disciplining, your actions using the power of track, target, and trim. Now you have it all. *If you commit yourself to track, target, trim, and train, you should never want for the material things in this world.* Now tell me the things I asked you to do to demonstrate your training proficiency."

I couldn't remember any of them except that I was supposed to read *The Wall Street Journal* and *Money* magazine.

"Maybe I had better get a piece of paper and write them down," I said. "Would you say them again."

"Checkmate," she said after making her last move. I tried not to show my disappointment in losing again. I borrowed a piece of paper from her desk and wrote down the things she wanted me to do to start my own money management training program.

By the time we met again, I had paid off all and destroyed all but one of the charge cards, paid off the overdraft balance, attended two investment seminars, read four books, and looked at six pieces of real estate. I was reading *The Wall Street Journal* at work rather than buying it, and was reading *Money* magazine at the library once a month.

Mary assured me we were not working on a quick fix for my financial worries. Nor were we talking about a get-rich-quick scheme that required no effort or risk. She said we were talking about change—a long-term change—developing a different way to look at money, changing the way I thought and acted in money matters, setting financial goals with more emphasis on debt elimination, and saving as opposed to getting more things.

"Most of us need to change the way we acquire and keep track of our money," she explained. "Most of us need to change the way we budget so we can live on less than we earn. Most of us need to change the way we spend, with more emphasis on buying the things that increase in value.

"Many of us carry a lot of emotional baggage, which makes these attitude and behavior changes especially difficult. We've inherited attitudes and behavior patterns from our parents. If Mom and Dad kept their financial papers in a box under the bed, we tend to do the same. If Mom grew up watching her mother hide money in a coffee can, she will probably do it too. If Dad bought whatever toy he wanted using the "I deserve this" rationale, the son will probably become a spendthrift too."

★   ★   ★

A young mother learned she had inherited her parents' hand-me-down attitudes about money:

"At thirteen, I was determined not to do the things my mother did that irritated me. Now I'm thirty-three, and I don't want to pass on to my daughter the thing I like least about my life—my financial situation.

"My husband, Mark, works hard and is a good father, but we aren't getting along. We have everything we want, just like my mom and dad. They had everything but peace of mind, and we're in the same boat.

"Mark wants to budget. Sounds gruesome to me. We need a solution before things get worse. We're so right for each other, and we get along so well. If it weren't for the money problems…

"I just had to have it all, now, just like Mom and Dad. But now I want so badly to be 'even' financially, that I am buying lottery tickets. I can't pass this on to my daughter.

"As a little girl, I cringed when my wardrobe was augmented with hand-me-downs. But now I punish myself because I've taken my parents' hand-me-down financial beliefs and allowed them to hurt me and my family."

It's time to change, if we haven't already. We live in a world that runs on money, so we might as well develop financially healthy attitudes and behaviors that will enable us to prosper in a world of money. Whether we like it or not, using money is something everyone has to do. We can use it foolishly and thoughtlessly and become slaves to it, or we can use it wisely, putting it to work for us, not only so we can enjoy the abundance and prosperity of the world, but also so we can be more effective in lightening the burdens of others.

I knew a student who wrote on his application for admission to business school that he wanted to learn how to earn and manage money so he would have the freedom in his life to do many things that had nothing to do with money.

The sad truth is that those who spurn money, and resist learning how to use it, often end up spending more time worrying about it than those who took the time early on to master the principles involved in acquiring, keeping, and managing money.

The people who understand money spend it on assets that generate wealth. Those who don't understand money, spend it on things that consume wealth, and thus the rich get richer and the poor get poorer. By following the principles outlined in this book, you can join the 10% of the people who provide the money for the other 90% to borrow.

Like in most of life's endeavors, basic principles are involved in getting and keeping money. Those principles can be learned in books, classes, and seminars, from counselors and advisors, and in the world of hard knocks. Some people claim they have made and lost several fortunes before they learned to preserve wealth.

Nobody has to go back to school, change careers, or buy a seat on the New York Stock Exchange. Learning about money is like driving a car. You may not aspire to drive in the Indy 500, but if you are to get along in this world, you must have sufficient skill with a car and sufficient knowledge of traffic laws to get to and from work and to be able to negotiate your way through a big city, on and off the freeways. You may not want to read *The Wall Street Journal* every day, or go to M.B.A. school, but anyone can subscribe to a financial newsletter, read an occasional money management book, even join an investment club that meets once or twice a month, or find a trusted financial advisor.

The basic principles involved in managing money are presented in this book. Track your daily expenses. Set targets. Live on less than you earn. Pay yourself first. Get out of debt. Get to where you are collecting interest instead of paying it. But there is much more to learn, especially after you get out of debt and are starting to look for places to put your money to work.

For example, one of the most dangerous fallacies among novice investors is that the rate of return is directly related to the amount of risk. The greater the risk, the greater the potential return. Sometimes this is true, but many times it isn't.

Suppose a marginal friend, who went through bankruptcy several years earlier, comes to you and wants to borrow $60,000. As collateral, he is willing to put up a free-and-clear piece of commercial real estate in the center of your town that he just inherited from the estate of an aunt. He has a recent appraisal on the property showing its value at $875,000. He is so excited about this new inheritance that he wants to take his wife on a trip around the world. That's why he wants to borrow the $60,000. Because of the potential complication of the bankruptcy causing a delay in getting a loan, he would rather get the money from you than from a bank. He wants to leave on the vacation in the next few days. He is willing to pay you 18% interest on the loan. He will pay you back in a few months, after he decides what he wants to do with the property.

If you had the cash, would you make the loan? Of course. Your risk is almost zero, and the return is twenty times what you are getting on your savings account at the bank. High return, low risk. Once in a while an opportunity like this comes along. But you can never take advantage of such an opportunity unless you have accumulated some liquid assets.

Success is defined as the place where preparation meets opportunity.

Is there such a thing as a low-return, high-risk investment?

The 4 Laws of Financial Prosperity

Sure. Suppose the boy next door decides to drop out of school to become a rock star. He asks you to loan him $60,000 so he can buy a new electric guitar, a lizard-skin suit, and a van with curtains on the windows so he can take your daughter with him to Los Angeles to make his first record deal. He says he'll pay you a 6% return on your investment, much more than what you are earning in the savings account. Low return, high risk. And he's mad when you say no.

Suppose a stock broker gets you all excited about buying pork bellies and other commodities on margin. He says a little bit of an upswing in demand can literally double your money overnight.

Tired of the low return at the bank, you give him the nest egg you have been feeding $300 a month for ten years, hoping you will double its value in a few days. A week later, when you call the broker, he tells you that instead of taking a gentle upswing, the market took a gentle downswing. Then there is silence on the phone. "What does that mean?" you ask. Then, in a matter-of-fact tone, he tells you all your money is gone. "You lost it all. Do you want to try again?"

Unfortunately, in school people receive more training on how to drive cars than how to handle money. Classes ought to be offered in "Personal Accounting" (tracking), "Financial Strategies" (targeting), "Budget Reality" (trimming), "Debt Management and Elimination," "Asset Accumulation I, II & III," "Real Estate for Dummies," "Asset Management," and "Protecting Your Nest Egg" (training). Each of these subject headings could be a four-credit-hour course, just for starters. There's plenty to learn, and if you're serious about getting control of your financial life, a certain amount of your time and resources should be allocated to education.

One dangerous pitfall for new investors is placing too much value in "hot tips" heard in the gym or restaurant. Everyone should have a trusted financial counselor. There are too many potantial pitfalls, and too much at risk, to make major financial decisions without counsel you can trust.

The Fourth Law

The first time you read this book, you might get the impression borrowing is bad. Not always. How many stories have you heard about people borrowing their way into a nice house or a big piece of land, only to see the value double in a few years, sometimes making hundreds of thousands of dollars for the borrower?

Borrowing for a home is one of the best investments anyone can make, but instead of paying it off in thirty years with two-thirds of your payments going to interest, save tens of thousands of dollars by paying it off in ten or fifteen years.

The young people who took out student loans twenty years ago so they could go to college are, for the most part, financially better off today than their counterparts who went to work out of high school. A study by the Governmental Commission on Mental Illness and Health concluded that there is a close relationship between years in school and the sense of well-being and satisfaction in life. The perspectives of college graduates were broader and aspiration levels higher. When they worried, their worries tended to be over genuine, not imagined, troubles, but no group escapes stress.

It's okay to borrow for things that increase in value. It's smart to borrow to buy a piece of real estate you think will double in value in two or three years. It may be smart to take out a $10,000 home improvement loan if the resulting improvements add $20,000 to the value of your home. It's even smarter to invest in your own future by getting the best education available in your chosen field. When preparation and opportunity come together, the result is success.

Borrowing for a car can be argued both ways. A car may depreciate in value, but you need reliable transportation to make a living. Just remember, borrowing to buy a good used car so you can get to and from work isn't the same as buying a $56,000 BMW with a 5% down payment.

There's a place in every financial plan where you forget all the talk about positive thinking, and develop a failure-avoidance strategy. Ask yourself, "How can I mess up?" This is when you realize that one medical disaster in a week could wipe out that $300 a month you have been saving for ten years if you don't have adequate health insurance. This is when you realize that if you suddenly died before the pension fund were fully funded, your spouse wouldn't have enough to live on if you didn't have life insurance. "What if, when I turn fifty, they decide to give my job to someone half my age? Could I reduce the chance of that happening with more training, or should I look at starting a small business on my own before I'm forced to do it?"

If you are paying more than 20% of your income in taxes (the average worker making $50,000 with two children and a mortgage pays 30% of his income in direct and indirect taxes), you might want to start looking at small- or home-business opportunities. A benefit of such a business may produce another $8,000 to $10,000 in legitimate tax deductions.

"If you are serious about preserving money, financial education and training should be an ongoing part of your financial strategy," Mary advised as she won another game of chess.

Training—the fourth law of financial prosperity.

We firmly believe the strength and prosperity of a nation or society depends largely on the strength and prosperity of its families.
—Blaine Harris

Tables Turned

After months of tracking, it was automatic, and we no longer missed the things we had trimmed out of our budget. I remembered Mary saying that while it may be possible to have anything you need, you can't have everything you want.

One evening when Mary and I got together for chess, I told her that when real estate agents tried to qualify me by asking how much money I had to invest, I told them I had a $2 million line of credit.

"I guess you do," she said. "As far as I am concerned you have satisfied your part of the agreement. How much of the $2 million do you want?"

"Maybe we better discuss it over a game of chess," I suggested. I didn't tell her I had read a book titled *Winning Chess Strategies* along with all the investment and real estate books.

While we were playing, I told her about the debts Judy and I had retired, and that we were now working on the home equity loan which was at 7%. Thanks to a couple of nice real estate commissions Judy had received, we were ahead of schedule on our Debt Eliminator program. I told Mary that since my first mortgage was 5.15%, I didn't really need any of the 8% money in the $2 million line of credit.

"Are you telling me you don't want my money, after all you've gone through to get approved?" She sounded surprised, shocked, even hurt.

"I'm not telling you I don't want it. I just don't need it now. My first financial goal is to get out of debt. Why would I want to incur more debt? Why would I want to go deeper in debt if I am on target to be out of debt completely in less than four years?"

"Maybe you'll need some help getting into a piece of real estate where you think you can double your money," she offered.

"In that event, I'll be knocking at your door asking for some of that 8% money," I said. Then I hesitated, stood up, and motioned for her to stand up too.

"I'm already so much in debt to you," I said as I put my arms around her. Tears were streaming from my eyes as I kissed both of her cheeks. "Thank you so much," I said, finally pushing her back so I could look into her tear-flooded eyes. She didn't say anything, but I could tell from her gentle smile that she was happy.

We resumed our game as I told her the story of the man who was walking along the beach at low tide. He noticed thousands of starfish lying on the wet sand, dying in the heat of the noonday sun.

"How sad," he thought, "that thousands have to die. It's too bad there are so many. One man cannot save them all."

The man continued his walk down the beach, and soon he passed a very old bare-footed woman who was picking up starfish, one by one, and throwing them back into the sea.

"My dear woman," said the strolling man. "Why are you throwing those starfish back into the sea? Can't you see there are many thousands? You can't even make a dent in the number of starfish that will die today. What difference are your efforts going to make?"

The old woman picked up another starfish and threw it into the sea, then replied, "It's going to make a difference to that one."

"That's a beautiful story," Mary said, "but why are you telling it to me?"

"Because I'm the starfish; you are the woman who threw me into the sea, and I want to thank you for doing it."

"Oh yes," I added. "There is one more thing."

"What?" she asked.

I reached down and moved my queen. "Checkmate," I smiled.

*One of the most powerful forces in the universe
is compound interest.*
—Albert Einstein

Interest

Mary probably thought she wouldn't see me anymore, now that I didn't need her money. But she was wrong. She had opened a whole new world of opportunity for me, and I was determined to learn all I could from her. We continued to play chess, usually two or three times a month. Usually she won, but I won too, because I always came away with some new idea or understanding that would help me along my way to financial prosperity. Interest became one of our favorite topics of discussion.

Interest is a formidable opponent. Once the game starts, he never rests. You may work 50 or 60 hours a week to keep up with him, but he works 168 hours a week to keep ahead of you. He never takes a timeout or a half-time break.

He works every Sunday, every holiday, and every night. He has no mercy. He even takes your money when you are sick in bed. And if you lose your job and miss payments, he will take your house.

The 4 Laws of Financial Prosperity

If you have a $220,000 mortgage on your home at 5.15%, you can go to sleep every night knowing over the 30-year mortgage you will accrue on average just under $600 per month in interest or about $20 a day. You pay $20 when you spend Christmas day at Grandma's. You pay another $20 every Saturday and Sunday, even if you aren't at work. When you signed the papers for that $220,000, 30-year mortgage, you agreed to pay $212,451 in interest. Add closing costs and occasional late fees, and you will pay for your house about two times by the time the mortgage is paid.

Everyone needs to know how much interest he or she is paying and be aware of the options available to drastically cut interest payments. For example, if you increased the payment on the above $220,000 mortgage by $533 per month, about $100 per week, it would enable you to pay it off in just over fifteen instead of thirty years. Your total interest expense would be $98,379 instead of $212,451, a savings of $114,072. That's a lot of money, enough to supplement your Social Security check very nicely after you retire.

And just think what that retirement would be like if you continue to pay yourself the equivalent of the mortgage payment, earning an 8% return, for the additional fifteen years. You would amass an additional $418,362 to enjoy during retirement. Don't forget, you have been living without that mortgage payment in your lifestyle for the past fifteen years. Now is the opportunity to really build wealth for you instead of for everyone else.

If you finance an expensive car over five years you will pay thousands in additional interest, even if you are financed at a very low rate because you have a great FICO score. And what about the 18% you pay on VISA and MasterCard, unpaid medical and dental bills, and so on? If you had a $5,000 balance on your VISA or MasterCard, and you paid the minimum payment of $125 a month, it would take about five years to pay the balance down to zero, assuming you never used the card again. During that time you would have paid an additional $2,693 in interest.

If you add up all the interest you are paying, including your mortgage, you can begin to see why you are struggling financially, even with a good job or a double income. Just think what you could do if you got to keep all that money you spend in interest every month. In my case, eliminating my interest payments was like getting a $1,200 a month tax-free raise.

I'm not suggesting that the bankers be hauled off to jail. If your banker helps you get into a fourplex apartment where your rental income is $4,000 a month, and your payment to the bank is $2,500 a month, and you'll own the thing free and clear in twelve years, that's a good deal, and you ought to give your banker a hug.

The general guideline for borrowing, endorsed by most financial planners, is that you borrow for things that increase in value or produce income, never for things that depreciate.

Borrow for business and to buy assets that increase in value, but pay cash for pleasure, comfort, and vanity.

For those who spend their way out of debt, interest can suddenly become a wonderful teammate. Instead of being a borrower, you are a lender. Instead of being in the interest trap, interest is working just as hard for you as it used to work against you. Twenty-four hours a day, seven days a week, it is earning money for you. It works weekends, holidays, and nights. It never takes a day off. It earns just as much for you on the days when you are sick as when you are well and just as much when you are on vacation as when you are working. Those who don't understand interest, pay it. Those who understand it, collect it.

Even with all Albert Einstein's great successes, he still said one of the most powerful forces in the universe was compound interest.

A person or couple earning a lifetime income of $2 million (about $45,000 a year), taking a 30-year mortgage and always paying minimum payments on bills, will pay $300,000 to $400,000 in interest.

Over a 45-year working career, $200,000 in interest breaks down to about $370 a month.

Suppose you invested $370 a month at 6% instead of paying it out. The amount you'd end up with is $1,024,816 in the bank when you retire. By continuing to earn 6%, you could withdraw $5,124 a month during retirement and never reduce the principal.

Now try this scenario. If you could come up with just another $30 a month and invest $400 a month for your entire working life, and earn an average of 9% interest on it, your nest egg would add up to $2,984,166 by the time you retire, and you could draw out $22,381 a month for the rest of your life, without reducing principal.

As you make modest increases in your savings, the impact over your lifetime will be dramatic. The point is that if you can just change the direction of your interest stream so it's coming in instead of going out, you will see wonderful, far-reaching changes in your financial life.

Mary was helping me get out of the interest trap, helping me make the transition from borrower to lender. And I was doing it without earning more money and certainly without robbing a bank or winning the lottery.

One reason most of us are borrowers instead of lenders is that we are too easily seduced by easy credit plans that make it possible to have the things we want now and not have to pay for them until later. Once we get on the interest/installment treadmill, it seems impossible to get off. Sure, we can get the things we want without having to pay up front, but is it worth it when we feel poor all the time?

Most of us can't afford to pay for our home two and half times, but we hardly hesitate signing documents to make sure we do just that. When we enter a store to buy something with an 18% APR credit card, if the clerk, upon seeing the card, automatically increased the price of the item by 50%, we probably wouldn't buy the item. But that is exactly the price we are paying, if we add the interest we will pay before the amount charged to the card has been paid off.

Too many people are already spending more than they earn each month, using three or four credit cards or home equity lines of credit to make up the difference. It isn't unusual for the outstanding balance on those cards to be over $10,000, requiring $150 a month in interest payments alone.

When we graduated from high school, most of us, including me, had dreams of making as much as we do now but thought we would be affluent and happy on that much income, not trapped in a frantic struggle from one paycheck to the next. We wonder why we had fewer money problems when we were earning a third of what we earn now. Worrying over money is more likely to cause high blood pressure than salt. Money worries sap vitality and break up families. Nothing robs us of our self-esteem quicker than bills we can't pay.

If the people in Bangladesh knew how much you and I were earning, they would call us Rockefellers. A college professor with a Ph.D. in Mongolia earns the equivalent of about $1,300 a month. Per capita income is only $18,170 USD per year in China, and they manage to save a higher percentage of their income than Americans do. We should count our blessings. Instead, we are frantically paddling a leaky canoe across an ocean of red ink, fearful that if we stop, the canoe will sink.

You may earn $2.5 million in your lifetime, but when you retire, if you're like the majority, you will have less than $100,000 in savings, not nearly enough when you are expected to live another fifteen years.

Each of us must immediately undertake the responsibility to make the necessary adjustments and train ourselves—and the upcoming generations—that our continual satisfaction of our never-ending spending appetite through the use of credit will ultimately produce a most painful result.

We are now living with the greatest technological and economic prosperity the world has ever known. While we enjoy this great power and potential, we must adjust our balance while the opportunity to do so is still there. We must develop an absolute abhorrence to waste and unnecessary spending.

So when are we going to learn that even though we can have just about anything we need, we can't have everything we want? When will we start treating our money as a precious resource?

An investment counselor was surprised when an aging couple, ninety-seven and ninety-eight years old, entered his office to see about starting payments into a retirement fund. "Why did you wait so long?" the counselor asked.

"Couldn't afford it while the children were alive," they responded.

The real tragedy is that many of the people in the interest debt trap didn't get there through ignorance and stupidity. Most of the Baby Boomers grew up in homes where they were taught, or at least observed, sound financial practices—paying off mortgages in years instead of decades, saving for rainy days, establishing savings accounts for college, putting money away for retirement.

If people know something about handling money, why don't they do it better? And if they don't know anything, why don't painful interest payments motivate them to take the courses, buy the books, and listen to the audios on getting out of debt and achieving financial prosperity?

Everybody wants to be out of debt. Everybody would rather collect interest than pay interest. Try to find someone who says he or she is perfectly content to retire on nothing more than Social Security. There are no such people. Then why are most of us headed for a place where none of us want to be?

If the know-how is available on how to achieve financial security, why don't people do it? Why do we find it so hard to resist all the convincing advertising aimed at getting us to buy things we cannot afford and don't really need? Why are we tempted by those offers for easy credit again and again? Why would we rather drive luxury sports cars now, than have $300,000 worth of mutual funds when we retire? Are we really that short-sighted?

Have you ever watched hungry children dig into big pieces of German chocolate cake? One child will eat the cake first and save the frosting until last. Another child will eat the frosting first, then the cake. Some like to save the best until last. Others eat the best part first. Adults are the same way. If you are going to watch a movie at home after eating dinner, do you clean up the dinner dishes before you watch the movie or after?

We're talking about delayed gratification, scheduling pain before pleasure, work before play, toil before rest. It's the way our parents and grandparents lived during the depression because bitter experience taught them it was the only way to survive. They had the old-fashioned belief that money should be earned before it could be spent. They were in a generation where one ate the cake before the frosting. We live in a generation where too many people eat the frosting first.

We believe the salesman when he says you might as well buy the item on credit so you can enjoy it while you are paying for it. What he doesn't say is that by buying on credit, if you add the interest to the cost of the item, you will be paying a much higher price for the item.

The business executive who puts the hard tasks at the top of his "to do" list and attacks them first accomplishes much more in a day than the person who saves the difficult tasks until last.

The 4 Laws of Financial Prosperity

Usually, he or she never gets to the more difficult tasks and, unfortunately, these are usually the most important items on any list. Delaying gratification is the process of scheduling the pain and pleasure in life in such a way as to make the pleasure better by facing the pain first and getting it over with.

People would rather go to movies, play basketball, go out to dinner, or just putter in the garden than work on finances— pay bills, balance registers, discuss budgeting and expenditure decisions. Such tasks are generally perceived as unpleasant, even painful, and because attention to personal finances is not required by law, except at tax time, such matters are either postponed or neglected altogether.

But if you stop and think about it, the discomfort associated in wrestling with financial problems now is nothing compared to the pain, hurt, and downright misery associated with foreclosure, bankruptcy, and facing years of retirement with nothing more than Social Security. With a little effort now, you can avoid a lot of pain later.

It's like the child who is having so much fun playing that he tries to ignore the growing discomfort in his bladder. He knows it's time to interrupt his play and go to the bathroom, but he's having too much fun. He continues to postpone the trip to the bathroom until what would have been only a minor interruption turns into a major inconvenience, requiring him to stop play altogether because he has to go home to bathe and find clean clothes.

Our instant gratification attitude will ultimately prove to be catastrophic. By learning to satisfy instant gratification desires with actions that create long-term benefits, we can turn catastrophe into reward and achievement.

This book presents better and more efficient ways to handle money. Too many people associate money management with unpleasant words like deprivation, denial, cutting back, belt-tightening, budgeting. It is just as easy to associate money management with pleasant words like spending, freedom, choices, dividends, peace of mind, and accomplishment. It is time we change the way we look at money. Buying mutual funds can be almost as much fun as buying a sports car.

Just about everybody reaches the point in life where they realize their income is about as high as it is ever going to get, and they are still a long way from feeling financially secure.

The truth is, you don't have to make a lot of money to become financially secure. All you need is a program that enables you to redirect the way you spend the income already in place, to a way that gets you out of debt and helps you accumulate sufficient assets to take care of you until the day you die. If this is what you want, following the principles presented in these pages will get you there.

Financial security is more about how you spend,
than how much money you earn.
—Blaine Harris

Spending

I reviewed my targets on a daily basis, and when each pay-check arrived, I paid myself first by taking 10% off the top to pay down the debt with the lowest remaining balance.

Once we were used to living on 90% of my income, we didn't even miss the other 10%. It didn't seem like very long at all until the home equity loan was paid off. The only remaining debt was the mortgage. Making double payments on the house and investing the rest made me feel like a victorious military general at a hero's welcome.

About this time, I surprised Mary by announcing that I wanted to write a book that would contain all the things she was teaching me. I was sincere when I told her that other people deserved the opportunity to know and understand the four laws too, and I thought the best way to share would be in the pages of a book.

"What makes you think a furniture salesman can write a book?" she asked. Her question didn't catch me by surprise. I had been asking myself the same thing for about a month.

The 4 Laws of Financial Prosperity

"You should see the love letters I write to Judy," I teased. We both laughed. Then I got serious. "It's not like I'm trying to write circles around Michael Crichton or scare Steven King to death," I said. "All I want to do is write down the things I learned from you so others can learn. I had to do a little bit of writing to graduate from college. I got A's in some of my English classes, and I'm an avid reader. I believe I can do it. Tom Clancy sold insurance before he hit the best-seller lists. John Grisham was a lawyer."

"Someday they'll be saying Paul Smith was a furniture salesman," she added. "What will you call the book?"

"*Spending Your Way to Wealth,*" I said, expressing the idea that creating wealth is not so much a function of budgeting and belt-tightening as it is the result of spending differently, spending your money to get out of debt, and investing in assets that appreciate.

"I don't know if I like it," Mary said. "First of all, it sounds too much like *Eating Your Way to Thinness.*"

I reminded her that there are diets in which people lose weight not by eating less, but by eating differently. They make changes in the kinds of foods they eat—less gravy, French fries, ice cream, and prime rib; more broccoli, grapefruit, cottage cheese, sprouts, and fish.

Spending, like eating, involves an infinite number of choices. At home and at school we tend to spend a lot of time teaching fundamentals of music, athletics, mathematics, reading and other disciplines, but we do not do a very good job of teaching our children the basic spending principles needed for financial survival in a world of money.

"Almost anyone with steady employment, regardless of income level and upon learning correct spending principles, can spend his or her way out of debt and achieve financial prosperity," Mary said. "When you buy something of value, you receive an instruction manual telling you how to care for that product to insure maximum use and longevity. But have you ever heard of an employer giving out instruction booklets with paychecks?"

I told Mary I always wondered why my paycheck never came with a set of instructions. The principles taught in this book are the instructions. The readers who follow the principles will be able to achieve debt-free prosperity while they are still young enough to really celebrate.

"Maybe we can show a few people that the financial dreams they didn't think were possible," she added, "are really within their grasp."

"After reading the book, they will have the tools to achieve those dreams," I added.

"In my years at the IRS, I saw some good money management, but more bad money management," Mary said. "A small number of families always seemed to have money available for college educations, down payments for children's homes, small businesses, and retirement, while most families with similar incomes always seemed to be struggling just to pay their bills, and never seemed to be more than sixty days away from bankruptcy.

"A book like this needs to be written," she added. "A handbook for paychecks that would show everyone, including our children, in a very logical and convincing way, how to get organized financially, how to get the most out of the money they earn, and how to get out of debt and become financially secure on any income."

The mission of this book is to help people achieve worthy financial goals by presenting well-conceived, easy-to-use methods for *tracking* expenses, setting *targets, trimming* expenses, and *training* readers in the art of spending money wisely. In this book, we reveal and teach the time-tested secrets used by normal people, at every income level, to achieve debt-free prosperity.

Financial security is more a function of how you spend than how much money you earn.

The 4 Laws of Financial Prosperity

Too many people have the false belief that the single biggest cause of financial stress is earning too little money. "If I only earned another $500 a month, I wouldn't have these problems."

What would happen if the President of the United States, during a reelection campaign, appeared on television one night to announce that, in order to relieve the financial pressure on individuals and families, he was ordering all companies, effective immediately, to give their employees a 10% across-the-board wage and salary increase?

What would be the consequence of such an action? The president would get reelected, for sure; but in six months, would there be less financial stress in America? No. Instead of using the extra 10% to pay off debts or increase savings, most people would take the extra money and make a down payment on a new Dodge truck or the boat they always wanted and increase their debt burden even more. *The lack of money doesn't cause as much financial stress as the lack of ability to spend our money wisely.*

Mary told me that years ago, she had a friend in Montana. His name was Mike, and he was building an attractive log home on one of the most beautiful hilltops in the scenic Bitterroot Valley. Mike was debt-free, and his only income was the hourly wage he earned at the Forest Service.

"When I got out of school, I landed a good job and spent every penny," Mike explained. *"But I wasn't happy, so I dropped out and became a hippie. I earned nothing and lived on nothing. I wasn't happy living that way, either. So I got another job, but continued living on nothing, like during my hippie days. I was driving a $150 car, and my wife bought clothes at Goodwill.*

"It wasn't long until I was able to buy 10 acres of good land," he continued. *"Then I started building the house, paying cash for the building materials. When it is finished, it will be mine. If I lose my job, I won't lose my house and land. In fact, if I lose my job, my land will provide for my family."*

He had an orchard, a large garden, chickens, and a cow. Mike worked hard, but enjoyed financial peace of mind.

Spending

We know a lot of people who say they would like to trade places with Mike. What they don't seem to understand is what Mike has is within the grasp of almost anyone with a steady job, as long as they understand they can have *anything* they need, but not *everything* they want. "Any fool can get money, but it takes a wise man to keep it," Mary added.

It takes management and discipline, the kind you have been reading about in this book. It's not as hard as you think. Help is available. The principles are simple.

1. *Track your daily expenses.*
2. *Target realistic financial goals, write them down, and imprint them in your internal computer.*
3. *Trim your living expenses so you live on less than you earn, then spend the difference to get out of debt and buy assets that appreciate. Pay yourself first.*
4. *Train yourself in the power of compound interest. Learn investment strategies for stocks, securities, and real estate. Develop a long-term relationship with a financial advisor and live the principles that govern wealth.*

Mary told me about a Vietnamese couple who arrived penniless in San Francisco in the mid-1980s. They obtained minimum-wage work in a donut shop. Being without any financial resources, they were allowed to stay in a back room. Leftover food was provided to them.

After several years, they had the opportunity to get an apartment. The American dream was finally within reach. But thinking it over, realizing that with the apartment they would have to pay utilities, buy a car, appliances, furniture, insurance, and groceries, they decided to stay in the back room and live on leftovers for two more years.

When they had been in the country five years, they bought the restaurant where they had been working. They paid $30,000 cash. They had saved 80% of the money they had earned. Today they own many restaurants.

Too many Americans spend 104% of their income, using

93

easy credit to go a little deeper in debt each month. Most American's have less than $5,000 in savings. Worrying about money is a leading cause of stress-related heart failure. Fighting about money is the leading cause of divorce.

Everybody seems so concerned about our precious natural resources—air, water, fossil fuels, rain forests, even whales and owls. But what about our money? Isn't it about time we started treating it as a precious resource? If you don't, you'll wish you had if you ever get a pink slip and have no reserve to fall back on, or when you get that gold watch and realize you'll be facing the golden years in poverty while your friends are spending their winters in Arizona and Florida.

Working harder and longer is not the answer. A new idea, a new way of doing business is needed. That's what this book is about.

It doesn't matter if you are earning $20,000 a year and feel like you are paddling a leaky canoe, or earning $200,000 a year and driving a sinking houseboat. The feeling is the same if you can't pay your bills and realize your ocean of debt is getting deeper and deeper. If you feel like you need a financial miracle and don't think you are going to win the lottery anytime soon, this book can show you what to do.

Most people have a very simple system for managing their money. They put their paycheck in the bank, pay the required bills, and they hope the rest lasts until the next paycheck. Of course, it doesn't. And when asked where the money went, they respond in broad, sweeping generalities because they have no clear picture of what happened to the money.

People seem to want to blame everyone else for their financial woes. "My employer is too cheap to pay a decent wage." "Shoddy government management is ruining Social Security." "Greedy landlords charge too much rent." "The IRS is stealing my money." "If American manufacturers were more concerned with quality than profit, I wouldn't have to spend so much money replacing all the stuff that breaks—I wouldn't be throwing away more dollars than people in India live on."

Who can you blame when you turn sixty-five and don't have enough saved up to get through a single year of retirement?

Who can you blame if the daughter you love so much wants to get a college education and you can't afford to help her?

If you don't know who to blame for your financial woes, look in a mirror.

It doesn't have to be this way. Responsible spending, regardless of your income level, can enable you to get the things you need and want.

The simple truth is that in the absence of a spending plan with clearly defined goals and a method of tracking money, people will spend whatever they earn, sometimes more, thanks to easy credit. The person earning $30,000 a year spends it all. The person earning $60,000 a year spends it all. The person earning $100,000 a year spends it all.

The first step in getting control of your spending is to start **tracking**, keeping a record of every dollar you spend on a daily basis and writing it down.

The next step is to set realistic **targets**. You can't create a plan to go somewhere if you don't know where you want to go.

Next, you have to **trim** your spending habits so that you live on less than you earn. You don't have to do like the Vietnamese couple and live on 20% of earnings, but if you can live on 85-90%, if you are typical, wonderful things can happen in your life.

If the $30,000-per-year wage earner forces himself to live on $27,000, he will hardly notice the difference. Likewise, the $60,000 wage earner won't have to give up much to live on $54,000, or the $100,000 person to live on $90,000. But they will all notice amazing changes in their financial problems. Their money worries will decrease because they have money in the bank and the knowledge that they are progressing toward desirable financial goals—getting out of debt, building a retirement annuity, saving for their daughter's college, etc.

And because they don't want to suffer setbacks through bad investments, they are constantly reading, asking questions, learning, and developing healthy financial habits. This we call **training**.

It is entirely possible for almost anyone on any income to live debt-free and to collect interest instead of paying it.

In the movie, *Sabrina,* starring Harrison Ford, the aging chauffeur, Fairchild, surprises his daughter with the announcement that, by staying home reading books and making careful investments over the years, he has accumulated over $2 million for her.

"Only in the movies," you might say. Not so. News reports on people like Fairchild are almost commonplace, like the one about a retiring postal worker who had accumulated $4.2 million in real estate investments. Or the cleaning lady who donated over half a million dollars to start a scholarship fund for needy African-American women.

When Anne Schreiber died at age 101 in 1995, *Money* magazine ran an article describing how this retired IRS worker had turned $5,000 in savings into a $22 million fortune, which she left to charity.

Eating is something we have to do every day. We can choose to do it well, or we can choose to do it poorly. By repeating poor habits daily, we can destroy things money cannot cure and we will pay for a lifetime. When we exercise the discipline to do it well, we enjoy the benefits for a lifetime. Money is no different. Small, daily good habits woven through the Track, Target, Trim, and Train principles will reap rewards for a lifetime.

Spending is like eating. We have to do it every day. We can't stop spending any more than we can stop eating. If we spend right, we can live debt-free with surplus money going into investment vehicles that pay for our children's educations and allow us to retire in comfort. On the other hand, if we spend irresponsibly, we always seem to be a dollar short, worrying about money, and with too little to retire on when we can no longer work.

As long as we are going to spend, we might as well do it right. *This book shows how anyone on any income can spend their way to debt-free prosperity.* Like Mary must have said to me a hundred times, "Now it's your move."

The ability to create wealth is a gift.
Improper management of the gift is ingratitude.
—Blaine Harris

More Money to Manage

"Paul, you are mastering the four laws and have proven to yourself that these financial principles not only work, but are essential for financial success.

"For some reason," Mary said, "most people believe that managing money in business is somehow more essential than managing the money that flows into a household. Just the opposite is probably more true, because if you learn to respect the value and power of properly managed money at home, you will probably be more responsible when it comes to the general waste and misuse of money anywhere.

"Paul, you have been a good student and I have enjoyed sharing the four most powerful financial principles in my life with you. You have demonstrated, once again, that anyone under virtually any condition can implement and immediately benefit from the proper application of these four laws."

I was pleased with my newfound financial confidence and was anxious to learn everything about building a strong net worth.

The 4 Laws of Financial Prosperity

"You have hinted to me that you had something else you wanted to share with me once I had demonstrated to you that I was committed to making the laws a part of my life. Do you remember what you were going to share with me?"

"Yes, I remember. Are you ready?"

I immediately replied, "If it has anything to do with money or my ability to move me faster and closer to my targets, I am more than ready."

Mary responded, "Paul, unfortunately many people have abused what I am about to share with you. They have chased the illusion that simply earning more money without a solid management commitment would create financial strength. They have never completely understood or perhaps never been taught properly the elements of the key principles you have learned so well. I know they have never been taught in our schools at any level. At the very least, the principles should be taught to every senior in high school before the world of 'wants' puts them on the wrong side of financial power. What I am about to share with you was understood so clearly by Benjamin Franklin in the mid 1700s.

"Do you know, Paul, Benjamin Franklin is on the $100 bill?"

"Really?"

"He was the first self-made millionaire in the new republic. He truly understood what he taught, because he achieved financial independence and international respect by applying this simple formula. He taught that there are two rules that must be applied by anyone in creating wealth. First, learn how to manage the money you already have and, second, create more money to manage.

"Paul, you have already started making Mr. Franklin's first requirement part of your daily thought process and actions, so let's take a few minutes and talk about his second.

"Most people have never created a financial-priority plan and, consequently, do not know how powerful an extra few hundred dollars a month really is. Since you have now stopped the financial leaks in your personal affairs, every new dollar you earn can be applied directly to achieving your highest priorities. For example, if a 35-year-old made a commitment to put $300 a month into a long-term mutual fund, averaging 10%, he would have nearly $1,000,000 in a retirement account at age 70 or $1,600,000 at age 75. Now if that same 35-year-old would earn enough extra money to invest $500 a month, he would have $1,750,000 at age 70, which would give him over $100,000 a year income at 6% and he would never have to touch the principal."

Additional income dramatically accelerates the realization of each of your priorities. Any emergency fund, college fund, vacation home, or retirement account grows rapidly with undiluted new income being applied directly to those accounts. By simply implementing the power of Ben Franklin's financial advice, many millionaires have been created. The sooner you begin, the less it requires. The power of the compounding effect of money is astonishing.

"Paul there are many ways for either you or your wife or both of you together to create whatever level of income is required to meet even your most extravagant dreams, as long as you maintain proper balance in your fundamental management plan.

"While you are learning to manage and master these four laws, you may be introduced to ideas and concepts that can produce for you dramatically more money to manage. You can create more money and at the same time implement everything you have been taught in order to take full advantage of the power of that new money. These laws will guide you as additional income flows into your control, directing each dollar to its highest and most effective use. Properly applied, these laws will create even more excitement and energy and will sustain you on your pathway to complete financial independence.

The 4 Laws of Financial Prosperity

"Now that you understand the compounding effect of additional income, which can come in many forms, accompanied by a determined commitment to financial management, let me teach you one more principle called regenerating income. When income is tied directly to labor, income stops when labor stops. When labor creates income that repeats itself, independent of additional labor, you will have created the most ideal form of income.

"As you generate new income, you will get a real and sustained rush as you see it go to work generating even more income while you are asleep or even when you're at the ball game. The yield you get from putting your money to work begins the powerful compounding effect of money earning money. With regenerating income, you not only get the benefit of your money making money for you, but now the labor you have invested to produce income is compounding on its own and is also making money for you. As this compounding income begins to grow and astound you, resist the urge to waste and spend frivolously. Instead, allow the fruits of your labor to grow, providing peace-of-mind, security, freedom, and choices for you, your family, and others.

"Whatever you do now, always be willing to share with anyone what you have learned, as freely as I have with you. You will find the more you share, the better you will feel, and the better you feel, the more energy you will generate to implement your own personal path to prosperity.

"God speed, my friend. Don't forget to share."

*Learning the disciplines necessary to manage small amounts
of money is the secret to the accumulation and
management of large amounts of money.*
—Blaine Harris

The 4 Laws

I'll never forget my last conversation with Mary. She was having serious heart problems, which were making it increasingly difficult for her to live by herself. She had decided to move to Oklahoma City to live with her daughter.

"This is your last chance if you want any of that $2 million," she said in a teasing voice. But I knew she wasn't teasing. If I wanted to borrow all or part of that money, I had no doubts about her willingness to give it to me.

"I'm going to miss you," I said.

"You'll do just fine. You've learned your lessons well. Now that you can't spend so much time playing chess with me, maybe you'll finish the book."

"I have a serious concern about the book," I said, moving over to the sofa and arranging the pawns on the board.

"Tell me about it."

"A book can't replace Mary Sessions," I said.

"What is that supposed to mean?"

The 4 Laws of Financial Prosperity

"I could never have gotten control of my financial life without your help."

"I know," she said, confidently.

"The regular meetings, going over the worksheets, making commitments, reporting back—a book can't do those kinds of things. For the readers to benefit as I have, they need a Mary Sessions."

"You're not suggesting that I let you put my name and phone number in the back of your book so ten thousand people will call me, asking for a $2 million line of credit?" she asked.

"No. I'm just afraid that if the readers don't have a Mary Sessions, they won't be able to do what I did."

"The principles are the same, whether they read them in a book or hear them while playing chess with me," she argued.

I had to agree. "But," I insisted, "once the principles are mastered, the key to applying them is consistency."

How many times have you been excited about a new diet, or exercise program, or learning a new sport or skill? You make a commitment to do it every day—only to be distracted a few weeks down the road. You remember a month later that you are no longer doing what you decided to do.

If you get into a Debt Eliminator program to be free of debt in three years, and you set aside an extra $200 a month for accelerated debt payments, if you forget to do it in the fourth and fifth months, how successful will you be in getting out of debt?

Mary said that the consistency we see in sports is the same kind required to be successful in any financial management plan. She said the power of compound interest reaches atomic proportions when a player is consistent, not just month after month and year after year, but decade upon decade.

Calvin Coolidge said, "Nothing in the world can take the place of persistence. Talent will not; nothing is more common than unsuccessful men with talent. Genius will not; unrewarded genius is almost a proverb. Education will not; the world is full of educated derelicts. Persistence and determination alone are omnipotent. The slogan 'press on' has solved, and always will solve the problems of the human race."

If the market continued to return its historical average of 10%, a 15-year-old can accumulate a million dollars by retirement by saving $35 a month. A 13-year-old can amass $2 million by retirement by putting away $2 a day.

If every teenager were required to read this book, some would start savings programs. But for every hundred that did, after six months, only two or three would still be doing it. It is human nature to slip back into old, sometimes fatal, habits.

Mary said the best way to ensure consistency in staying on a financial path to prosperity is to focus your energy, your thinking, and your actions on the reward of what's most important to you. Life is to be enjoyed. The fallacy is that the only way to enjoy it is to spend, spend, and spend. Give yourself a chance to feel the success of being in control of your money rather than being controlled by it. One success leads to another and before you know it, you will be enjoying not only the financial rewards, but also the emotional rewards of ridding your life of unnecessary stress and baggage due to financial mismanagement. Once you have experienced the exhilaration of being a leader in the financial game of life, you will never go back to being on the other side of the coin!

The discipline necessary to achieve success in anything in life is not difficult because it is a by-product of targets to which one is passionately committed to. Behavior modifies itself to accomplish the thing that is most passionately and urgently on the mind. Don't trade what you want most in life for what you want right now. Keep your eye focused on your highest priorities.

Mary continued, "Private individuals can now receive instant feedback and clearly defined pathways taking them step by step from where they are today to where they most desire to be. Interactive Web applications can help you implement each of the four laws and assist you on your path to success," Mary said.

"And by the way, Checkmate!"

"Did you say Checkmate?" Paul replied.

"Yes, you've heard me say that almost every time we've played chess," she smiled. "Remember, life, like the game of chess, requires us to think several moves ahead and plan our strategy to ultimately put us in control."

I had to laugh, thinking how ironic it was that Mary always seemed to find a way to win our chess games, and in the process, she positioned me to win a much bigger game!

The 4 Laws—positioning you to
win the financial game of life.

The Financial
Wellness Challenge

We challenge each of you to make a difference. We are each on the chessboard of life. We must assume the responsibility for ourselves and those who depend on us, and make them our number-one priority in life. We must then manage our activity with absolute intensity, which must drive every move we make in order to achieve self-reliance and complete financial independence.

We challenge you to spend the next little while doing what most people won't, so you can spend the rest of your life doing what most people can't.

The next move is yours...

Authors' Final Thoughts

With this final chapter, we feel impressed to remind you of a couple of overall thoughts as you take what you have been taught and witness for yourself a remarkable transformation in your ability to master the power of money.

We like to think of this book as a "Cash Coach" or "Cash Coach in a Can." It doesn't matter whether you have just bought the finest set of golf clubs available or own the most efficient kitchen known to man, if you don't use them with some degree of commitment to improve, it has been for naught.

Transmitting coaching energy and deep believability into script is difficult at best. These pages were written to make bad money managers good and good money managers better. The power of Priority Thinking™ is just beginning to be understood by the great teachers and coaches of the world. We know that when the mind can select without undue outside pressure to choose and can begin to visualize the emotion and feeling associated with fulfillment, then behavior conforms, as it must, to the overpowering influence that comes from clear priority thought.

Paul has just started to master the power of the four laws of priority thinking and you have just been given an eagle's view of the most exciting, peaceful, and stimulating new principles, that will separate you from those old and unproductive thoughts and habits.

If you have arrived at this new point in your life with a greater desire to become financially free from your past limitations, you will witness the unveiling of great financial truths to create wealth. The influence of the fourth law, "Training," is just about to be revealed. Your priority-thought process will selectively drive your behavior to fulfillment and lead you to stimulating and accomplished successful people who will continue to train you and motivate you to realize the great priorities of your life. You will be given opportunities to create new wealth, which you must embrace with great commitment and dedication. More money will become available to you through the priority process that you must, at all costs, cause to conform to the power of the four laws, which have just been revealed to you.

Learn now with excitement, as you cause yourself and those about you to become more proficient as your money, talents, and assets respond to the priorities of your life. Money will respond to your command much like animals to the greatest of trainers.

Thank you for your enthusiasm to learn and to progress. Great prosperity and peace of mind will now be yours.

The next move is yours!

About the Authors . . .

Blaine Harris has spent most of his life creating, managing, and consulting with businesses. He has served as the CEO and chairman of the board of many private and public corporations, both nationally and internationally.

Blaine's greatest thrill in business comes from the association with men and women who are passionately committed to the purpose of the business. He is energized as he shares his vision of business and success to those who are eager to learn and improve. Having grown up in a construction family, he has owned, developed, and managed apartments, warehouses, shopping centers, condominiums, and subdivisions. He was the cofounder and past CEO and chairman of the board of an international business which became *Inc. Magazine's* highest-performing franchise of the year.

Blaine's faith in God, his family, country, and business are his greatest loves. He loves any outdoor sport. His personal preference is riding motorcycles. He currently is a contributing member of The Financial Wellness Group, whose mission it is to improve the quality of life of individuals and families through the management of money and the implementation of fundamentally simple principles of truth basic to success everywhere.

Charles Coonradt, chairman and CEO of The Game of Work, Inc., is internationally recognized in the fields of productivity and profitability improvement as an author, consultant, and speaker.

Chuck's books *The Game of Work* and *Managing the Obvious* have been labeled the most original and useful tools for business to come along since *In Search of Excellence.* He is a contributing author to the *Chicken Soup for the Soul* series.

111

Chuck's clients include PepsiCo, Fleming Companies, Marker Bindings, Hoechst Celanese, Ralston Purina, Browning-Ferris Industries, and many other Fortune 500 firms. Over one million managers and supervisors have heard Chuck's unique message. He lives with his wife and children in Park City, Utah.

Appendix

Charts associated with the "Debt-Free" chapter.

Itemized Debts

	Debt 1	Debt 2	Debt 3	Debt 4	Debt 5	Debt 6
Balance						
Payment						
Interest						
# Pmts.						

If you would like to process your custom Debt Eliminator program online, visit www.thefinancialwellnessgroup.com and enroll for the Debt Down online system. You can use the Debt Eliminator Input Sheet found on page 115 to organize your debt information for input.

Appendix

Debt Eliminator Worksheet

Month	Debt 1	Debt 2	Debt 3	Debt 4	Debt 5	Debt 6	Pmts.
Aug. 20xx							

Appendix

DEBT ELIMINATOR
INPUT SHEET

Extra Cash Applied to Debt Eliminator: _____

Annualized Return on Investments: _____

Description	Interest Rate	Amount Left	Monthly Payment

115

Comments   **Page No.**

Notes

Comments   **Page No.**

About FranklinCovey

(Co-publisher of *The 4 Laws of Financial Prosperity*)

At FranklinCovey, our mission is to enable greatness in people and organizations everywhere. We believe the outcomes of great organizations include:

- Achieving sustained superior financial performance.
- Creating intensely loyal customers.
- Developing a winning organizational culture.
- Making a distinctive contribution.

Through a balanced focus on individual effectiveness, leadership development, and processes that drive focus and execution, we believe organizations can achieve these outcomes—predictably and measurably.

FranklinCovey Co. (NYSE: FC) is a global company specializing in performance improvement. We help organizations achieve results that require a change in human behavior. Our expertise is in seven areas: leadership, execution, productivity, trust, sales performance, customer loyalty, and education. FranklinCovey clients have included 90 percent of the Fortune 100, more than 75 percent of the Fortune 500, thousands of small- and mid-sized businesses, as well as numerous government entities and educational institutions. FranklinCovey has more than 40 direct and licensee offices providing professional services in over 140 countries.

For more information, visit www.franklincovey.com.

Services and Products

- *The 4 Disciplines of Execution* consulting services
- *The 7 Habits of Highly Effective People* Signature Program
- *The 5 Choices to Extraordinary Productivity* work session
- *The 4 Roles of Leadership* work session
- *The Leader in Me* products and work session
- *Project Management Essentials for the Unofficial Project Manager* work session
- *Writing Advantage, Presentation Advantage,* and *Meeting Advantage* work session
- And more

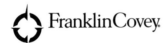 **FranklinCovey.**   2200 West Parkway Blvd.
Salt Lake City, UT 84119
(801) 817-1776

www.franklincovey.com

We enable greatness in people and organizations everywhere.

119

THE ULTIMATE COMPETITIVE ADVANTAGE

FranklinCovey is a global company specializing in organizational performance improvement. We help organizations achieve results that require a change in human behavior.

Our expertise is in seven areas:

LEADERSHIP

Develops highly effective leaders who engage others to achieve results.

EXECUTION

Enables organizations to execute strategies that require a change in human behavior.

PRODUCTIVITY

Equips people to make high-value choices and execute with excellence in the midst of competing priorities.

TRUST

Builds a high-trust culture of collaboration and engagement, resulting in greater speed and lower costs.

SALES PERFORMANCE

Transforms the buyer-seller relationship by helping clients succeed.

CUSTOMER LOYALTY

Drives faster growth and improves frontline performance with accurate customer- and employee-loyalty data.

EDUCATION

Helps schools transform their performance by unleashing the greatness in every educator and student.

About The Financial Wellness Group™

Our mission at The Financial Wellness Group is to help individuals and families take control of their money and build financial prosperity. For more than a decade we have been training and providing financial wellness solutions to individuals, families, groups, companies and universities based on our proprietary "4 Laws" principles. These principles break the complexity of money into four powerful, yet easy to implement steps that anyone can learn, remember, and implement. These simple steps lead to:

- Reduced financial stress.
- Elimination of debt.
- Increased savings and investments.
- Achievement of financial goals.
- Greater financial security and strength.

To learn more about how you or the clients you serve can benefit from our products, training, and services, visit us at www.thefinancialwellnessgroup.com or call us at (801) 296-6300.

The Next Move Is Yours!

121